"The

A Handbook on C  **elief**

Miercinga Theod
Little Elm, TX, USA

Dedicated to Garman Lord for envisioning what would become Þéodisc Geléafa.

With a special dedication and great deal of thanks to Gerd Groenewold, Wulfgæst, Êrmund, Tee Wódening, and Eric Wódening for making Þéodisc Geléafa what it is today.

Contents

Foreword

Þéodisc Geléafa or Theodish Belief (as Þéodisc Geléafa has been known for much of its history) is "the belief of the tribe." Its basis is the idea that ancient Heathenry was tribal in nature, and therefore the best way to worship the ancient Germanic Gods and Goddesses is in a tribal society. Here is not the place to make a case for tribal worship that will be done in Chapter II. However, leave it to say, that Theodish Belief has changed and evolved a great deal since Garman Lord first formulated it in 1976 much less since the publication of his book The Way of the Heathen.. Most of this change has occurred as Theodish groups such as Sahsisk Thiod, Axenhof Thiad, New Anglia, and the Miercinga Theod sought out more authentic or traditional practices, rites and beliefs of the historical Germanic tribes (as opposed to our fantasies about them).

Much of the earlier Theodish "template" brought forth by Garman Lord, while created with good intent, did not reflect historical reality. Without acknowledging historical reality, one cannot truly get in touch with the tribalism of ancient times. Without getting in touch with ancient tribalism, one cannot worship the Ése (Æsir) and Wen (Vanir) in a way close to the ancient Germanic tribesmen would have (one can effectively worship them no doubt, but they cannot do so and be Theodish). Thus, various Theodish groups dedicated themselves to scholarly study of the ancient Germanic tribes, particularly the ones they wished to revive, and as a result, Theodism evolved and changed, and with it, its core beliefs and practices.

As such, you will see nothing in this work about Greater or High Theodism. With all regard to Garman Lord, those definitions have no bearing on Theodish Belief today. A group is either Theodish, or not Theodish, there is no in between. What makes a group Theodish? What are the criteria? These are not just questions asked by non-Theodsmen. They are the very questions asked by the leadership of Theodish groups of each other. The only truly agreed upon criterion for being Theodish is that a group truly tries to revive the custom, culture, and societal structure of an ancient Germanic tribe. Some groups that claim to be Theodish do not fit this criterion due to problems in some area. Others that are not Theodish would fit this criterion with a few minor changes. Another criterion acknowledged by a majority of the accepted Theodish groups is simple acceptance by the established Theodish groups as being Theodish. The only thing truly agreed upon is that a single individual cannot be Theodish. Being Theodish requires a tribe.

With all that in mind, one can see that defining Þéodisc Geléafa is not a simple matter. With only a few exceptions, one cannot point to any one certain set of beliefs and say, "this is Theodish." From theod to theod, societal structures are different, thews or virtues are different, custom and tradition are different, rites are different, even some times Gods are worshipped by one tribe that are not another. Some theods plan eventually to enact sacral kingship. Others, because of customs of the ancient tribe they are reviving may rely solely on a council of aldermen. This is as it should be as it truly reflects ancient Heathen reality. The beliefs of Þéodisc Geléafa are tribe or theod specific. And while one may be able to list things the ancient Germanic tribes had in common, such as assemblies, many of the major Gods and Goddesses, a belief in Wyrd, a structured society....one cannot make hard and fast statements about their beliefs, society, or rites, that would be true of all the tribes. Each Germanic tribe had its own culture, its own dialect, and its own deities even as early as 2500 years ago. Each one entered history as unique. For this reason, modern Theodish groups are going to be unique unto themselves, and commonalities will not always hold for all.

Because of this, Theodsmen are apt to become scholarly sorts (amateur and professional) reading anything and everything that might give them clues to the ancient customs of their theod. They generally study not just their own ancient theod, but also other ancient theods, so they can better interact with other Theodish organizations. A good Theodsman can be a theologian, anthropologist, archaeologist, sociologist, priest, leader, husband or wife all rolled into one (reminiscent of Heinlein's words "specialization is for insects"). They become experts of comparative studies to fill in gaps. Sometimes, information that has not survived to come down from one ancient tribe will have come down to us from another. When you really come down to it, Theodish Belief is all about being true to one's ancestors or adopted ancestors. One tries to be as authentic as possible while adapting the ancient beliefs and practices to a degree to the modern world (the belief in Wyrd for example translates well to the modern world, human sacrifice does not). So long as a group does this, they may be thought of as Theodish. Those that use later medieval practices, feudalism for a social structure, obviously Christian viewpoints,

Neo-Pagan practices for rites, while they may be called Heathen, are not Theodish. It can be that simple.

The way of the Theodsman is one of the retro-heathen. Retro-Heathenry was defined by Garman Lord in the early `90s as Heathenry that attempts to authentically reconstruct ancient Heathenry. It differed from Arch-Heathenry, in that Arch-Heathenry was only possible prior to the Conversion, and therefore was a pure form of Heathenry. It also differed from Neo-Heathenry in that Retro-Heathenry sought to be true to its roots in the ancient religious cultures of the Germanic tribesman. Theodism is a form of Retro-Heathenry. Other forms may exist today, but Theodism is by far the most visible.

However, the purpose of this book is not to define Theodism, but to give a truer, more faithful view of "what it's all about." There are many misconceptions about Theodish Belief. Many of these misconceptions are because many still cite obsolete works such as Garman Lord's The Way of the Heathen as an authority on Theodish Belief (please note this is not to degrade this work, it was in its day, the greatest work on Theodism, but, the fact is it is badly outdated). Other misconceptions are because not all Theodish groups have gone the same direction as the majority, but have stayed with older, unauthentic forms of Theodism, thus placing them outside the current definitions of Theodish Belief. In addition, critics of Theodish Belief propagate other misconceptions, not caring whether the information they hand out is accurate or not. I hope this book can remove the confusion. I am indebted to the other

Theodish leaders who have supplied information helpful to writing this book, and for defining Theodism as it is, not as it was.

Theodish Belief, in its purest form is a beautiful thing. It can provide order, spiritual deepness, and security to one's life. It gives fellowship, a consistent belief system, and answers to how to handle many of the world's problems in a way many Neo-Pagan traditions cannot. There is magic, ritual, and deeds behind its very core, not to mention the faithful worship of the Ése (Æsir) and Wen (Vanir). Two thousand and five hundred years ago, Heathenry knew a diversity as rich as that of Hinduism. Its philosophy, its beliefs, its rites had as much depth as Buddhism. Had it not been for the greed of a few traitorous rulers, and the tolerance of the folk, Heathenry may have survived to this day. And, had it, it may well have survived with the tribal cultures that were the norm for ancient Heathenry. Theodish Belief therefore is a "what if." What if the Conversion, had never happened? What if the ancient tribes, had survived into Modern Times? The groups that follow Theodish Belief cannot claim to be survivals of the ancient tribes. The only way Theodish Belief differs from other modern Heathen ideologies or philosophies is that instead of just taking the deities and rites of the ancient Heathens and applying them to the modern world, Theodish Belief tries to take much more. Theodism is about reviving not just the worship of the Heathen Gods and Goddesses, but also the entire belief system and social structure of the ancient tribes, to take all it can of the ancient mental culture. Modern culture is in many ways corrupt. It has lost many of its benefits that were apparent as late as one hundred years ago. Gone are many of the folk beliefs of yesterday, along with the idea of family, honor, and community. Theodish Belief therefore tries to bring back the beauty and splendor known by the ancient Heathens as they interacted as individuals, families, and tribes.

A word on language usage, this book uses Old English as its primary form for ancient terms. Where it does not, this will be noted. All terms that are from one of the Old Tongues will be in italics. Other specialized terms developed by Theodish Belief over the years will not, nor will terms commonly used in modern Heathen terminology (but from an ancient language nonetheless) such as symbel will not be italicized.

Finally, this book was written for someone familiar with Germanic Heathen beliefs and concepts. If you are new to Germanic Heathenry, perhaps you should obtain a copy of my book *Hammer of the Gods: Anglo-Saxon Paganism in Modern Times*, or James Coulter's *Germanic Heathenry*, to help you understand the terms and concepts used here.

Chapter I: What is Theodish Belief?

Keeping in mind that we cannot truly define Theodish Belief with any precision, an attempt will be made to explain the reasoning behind Theodish Belief. Þéodisc Geléafa (as Theodish Belief is also called) means in Old English "tribal faith"; it is the "belief of the tribe." Two thousand years ago had someone asked a Germanic tribesman what their faith was, they would have explained their religion as the belief of the folk or tribe. Tribes at that time were social units linked by a common cultural identity, common history, as well as shared customs, traditions, and religion. Often Germanic tribes traced descent from a common ancestor, usually a hero or even a deity. Tribes gave their folk very much a sense of community and identity. Social bonds within the elder tribes were usually one of blood (tracing back to the common forebear), adoption, or via hold oath (an oath similar to blood brotherhood in that it bound two people together), and were much stronger than the bonds of general society today.

The great sociologist Emile Durkheim, found that loss of social identity or cultural identity within a society generally lead to a decline in morale within the individuals of that society. Such a loss of morale could lead to depression and suicide, and therefore societies that over emphasize individualism, were prone to higher suicide rates than those that emphasized cultural identification while still maintaining individual rights. Societies with little to no regulation of individuals, and with no social structure according to Durkheim were also those that see a decline in morals, an increase in

11

crime, as well as depression and suicide. Ideally, Durkheim thought that the only way to combat this was to reintegrate individuals into some form of social structure. In a similar vein, the great Chinese philosopher Confucius felt that social order came from respecting the custom and traditions of society, respecting humanity (or Jen), and proper behavior towards one's ancestors and the living (or the concept of Li). Thus, Þéodisc Geléafa seeks to rebuild tribal societies in order to create a healthier society, one with social order and harmony.

Þéodisc Geléafa therefore holds that the natural place for Germanic Heathenry and the worship of the Germanic Gods and Goddesses is in a tribal society. The ancient Germanic peoples from time immemorial worshipped the deities as a community; either as families, clans, or tribes. They were social creatures and while individuals had many of the rights they do today, these were often secondary to the concerns of one's tribe. While it would be difficult to form tribes now as they were in elder times, Theodish Belief seeks to reform them in such a way that at least some of the benefits of tribalism will be felt.

Theods generally hold certain beliefs in common (but not necessarily all of them). Amongst these social concepts are:

a) Sacral leadership, the idea of a sacral ruler that collectively holds the luck of the tribe.

b) A tribal assembly, a place where the folk can make law and discuss problems.

c) A structured society, one which has distinct social classes in which one has to learn their position; that all have freedom of conscience, and finally, that folk can be bond together by oaths and blood into a tribe.

There are other concepts Theodish groups hold in common. These are a belief in Wyrd, certain very generalized customs such as the use of wergild (though how this is handled will vary from group to group), the idea of giving to the Gods and getting gifts in return, frith and grith (peace within the tribe and between tribes respectively), and general thews concerning conduct of one's self. This list is not all inclusive. There are many other things that all Theodish groups may have in common. However, often when dealing with Theodism it is better to be on the conservative side when trying to identify what theods may or may not have in common.

This begs the question, why try to reconstruct, revive, or reawaken (choose your term) ancient tribes? Why not just create new tribes? One could indeed make new tribes, with no doubt, a great deal of success. However, there are advantages to using an ancient tribe as a basis. The least of these is some consistency of belief, practice, and social norms. Anyone starting a new tribe will have to create a whole set of customs, laws, a social structure, and many other constructs in order to achieve the status of a tribe. This is not wrong, but just difficult. Those that are trying to do that deserve admiration. However, part of being a theod or tribe is holding many beliefs, customs, traditions in common. It means a common history and identity about which there is no to little doubt. Reconstructing an ancient tribe provides these things much easier than creating a new one. If I say I am an Englisc Theodsman (in the sense I follow the ways of the ancient Angles), one has a reference point to what culture I may feel I am a part. They may know the history of the Angles, what few beliefs survived, and what names I may call on the Gods by. By using an ancient tribal sidu (Old English for custom or tradition), we provide ourselves with a starting point for a tribe to evolve from. Someone that creates a new tribe will also be providing a starting point, but that starting point will require much work to create. Ancient tribes, if any history remains about them, provide nearly everything one would need or want to lay a foundation for a modern tribe. Theodsmen do not think or feel they are the ancient tribe they are reconstructing, but that they are a part of a new tribe using an ancient tribe as a foundation.

The foundation provided by using an ancient tribe lays in its common identity. Many people living today can either trace themselves ancestrally or culturally back to an ancient Germanic tribe. If one is living in the English speaking world, they have a link of some form to an ancient Germanic tribe through ancestry, language, or culture. People in Canada, England, Australia, not to mention other places, start with a common identity to work from. An ancient tribe also gives a common history. Anyone that decides to join say, a theod dedicated to the ancient Frisians can sing the glories of the ancient Frisian king Radbod.

The history of an ancient tribe is its *orlæg* (Old English for a concept much like karma). And, it can be said that by adopting an ancient tribe's name, the members of that theod are inheriting that tribe's *orlæg* (much as amongst the Dark Age Norse children named for ancestors were thought to take on that ancestor's *orlæg*). Finally, an ancient tribe provides a theod with common thew (archaic modern English for virtues, customs). Holding values in common is important for any group, be it the Lion's Club or a nation such as the United States. Groups without common values are likely to fracture at the first sign of crisis (much like the United States is currently experiencing a decline). Theodsmen do not automatically take on the identity, history, and values of an ancient tribe though. It is a long process, which can take years to complete. This process can be broken down as follows:

a) Learning: In this stage, the Theodsman learns all they can about the culture of the tribe they are reconstructing. A culture's belief system is hidden not just in its writings. Coded into the very words it uses, the structure of its language, the artwork it uses to depict the world, even its clothing are the beliefs and the world view of a culture. A Theodsmen therefore, may take on the study of the Old Tongues of the Germanic tribe they are reconstructing (for example, Old English, Old Norse, Gothic), take up a craft that requires they recreate the artwork of the ancient Heathens (albeit often with modern tools), they may even dress like the ancient Heathens for worship. Thus, the learning stage is much more than just reading and memorization. It is an attempt to synthesize what they are learning. It is a process of ridding one's self of all they have known before, and taking on new beliefs, new values, even to a degree a new identity. In order to reconstruct authentically, a tribe, one must first get to know that tribe, become intimate with its identity, history, and values. A Theodsman in this stage is generally in a probationary membership status or apprenticeship. As such, in addition to book learning and the above, they may be required to serve the tribe in order to know how to place the tribe often above themselves.

b) Enacting: This is when the Theodsman begins applying what they have learned. They begin to apply the values of the ancient tribe in daily life (although often adapted to account for the differences between the theod's values and that of the host culture), worship much as an ancient Heathen would, and believing as an ancient Heathen would. Enacting is not an easy process, and may take years. It is, as much a learning process as anything. One can read about riding a bike. One can study the physics of it, and work out mathematically how it works. They can look at what muscle groups one uses when riding. Even ride a tricycle to learn how to pedal. But, until one learns to ride a bike, they cannot say they have become a bike rider. The same is true of being a Theodsman. One can learn about an elder tribe, learn its language, values, its religion, but until one actually uses that knowledge, they cannot be called a Theodsman.

c) Becoming or Worthing: Becoming is just that, becoming. One becomes a Theodsman. The easiest way to define this final stage is that it is the point one reaches when they are wholly Heathen. They have Heathen ideas about the world, Heathen virtues, and Heathen beliefs. They are as close as one can come to an ancient

Heathen living in the modern world. This stage never truly ends. As soon as one thinks, they know all there is about the rites, the Gods and Goddesses, Wyrd; some event may happen that changes it all. Unlike learning and enacting, becoming is not based in rational, objective observation or action, although that plays a part. It is a very subjective process, and as one changes and the world changes about them, so will their ideas change. For a few, this leads them out of Theodism. For others it leads them out of Heathenry altogether. But, for still others, it means going deeper into what it means to be a Heathen. Theodsmen often call this stage, worthing. Worth, is not to be confused with the word of the same spelling meaning "value." This term is related to the elder word Wyrd, and is the process of laying deeds both good and ill in the Well of Wyrd. Deeds laid down in the well determine one's *orlæg*. One can think of *orlæg* as one's personal law of causality. It is the sum of all one has done, and therefore, it is what determines what results one gets in the present. If one fails to study for a test, they may fail if not prepared, and in the future, they may also fail tests as this is the *orlæg* one has laid down.

Thus, this threefold process is all about laying deeds down to make one's self Heathen. One may go through this process many times in their life as they constantly reevaluate their beliefs and ideas. The way we were raised (and for most that means in a Christian, Judaic, or other non-Heathen religious setting), old ideas, society at large all combat the process of becoming a Heathen and eventually a Theodsman (they are a part of our *orlæg* we must overcome). Many of the values of modern society are drawn from Christianity,

Humanism, Managerialism, and half a dozen other institutions or belief systems that are sometimes at odds with a Heathen, much less Theodish world view. In many ways, even the most learned, wizened, and experienced of modern Heathens knows less about Heathenry than a ten-year-old Heathen child 2000 years ago. Unlearning much of what we came into Heathenry with, therefore is a difficult process. We have to unlearn as much as we learn, and this requires constantly asking, "is this the Heathen thing to do, or am I just acting on something I learned that is not Heathen?" Worse is the question, "Am I doing this because I am Heathen, or because society at large tells me to?"

Thankfully, for Theodsmen, they do not have to go through this process alone. Within Theodish Belief, there is the support network of the tribe. Every member of a theod serves as mutual support for the other members. They help reinforce one's Heathen world view. Further, the common values of the tribe serve as a checklist as to what one should be doing as a Heathen. Theodish Belief provides consistency in behavior through mutual support, as well as common identity, history and customs.

This process is very similar to the one put forth by Edred Thorsson in his article "How to be Heathen." Thorsson's process went as follows: 1) Rational discovery 2) Subjective synthesis 3) Enactment (Thorsson, "How to be Heathen" Idunna vol. 4 issue 4). The only problem with Thorsson's process is that for many it is difficult to achieve subjective synthesis without first "going through the motions." Otherwise, it could apply just as well to the process of becoming a Theodsman. In some cases, Thorsson's process may better apply.

Finally, once one has undergone the process of becoming a Theodsman, they will reap the benefits of belonging. Part of being a Theodsman is belonging to a tribe, not in the sense of being owned, but in the sense of being a member of something greater than one's self. Modern American culture truly is no culture at all. It has a common history, a common identity, but there are no shared customs, traditions, and religion. This leaves members of the society at large often confused as to how to handle themselves. Even when one does have a group such as a church where there are shared common values, the family is secondary to all else. Modern Managerialism has contributed to the destruction of the extended family by requiring people move away in order to work, thus eliminating the support given by one's extended family. Meanwhile, Christianity has actively sought to make the family secondary to the Church for ages. Without this support, the nuclear family also often falls apart due to divorce, further complicating the issue.

Within Theodism, both the extended family, and the nuclear family are very important. The nuclear family or *mægð* , is central to Þéodisc Geléafa. It forms the basis of the *sibb* , the extended family or clan (in the sense of the McCoy or Hatfield clans). The *sibb* consists of more than just the living members (counted out in some Germanic cultures to the fifth degree) but also all the ancestors. The ancient Germanic law codes rarely addressed individuals as concerns punishment. The smallest unit of these law codes was the *sibb* . If an individual did wrong, the living *sibb* had to pay wergild (a fine for murder), not the individual. In addition, the individual potentially offended the ancestors of the *sibb* as well. In any ancient Germanic tribe, it was the *sibb* that formed its core (not, contrary to popular belief, the *dryht* or warband). As late as one hundred and fifty years ago, families took care of their sick, elderly, and children, and this is how it was in ancient times. While it is rare that entire families will be Heathen, much less, Theodish, the *sibb* and *mægð* are very important, and with time, there will be entire families that will be Theodish. They are what provide an identity to an individual, and provide the most support. Beyond this, all the members of the theod also provide support to its members. A theod is very much a support group for its folk. It is a culture, or subculture, or an attempt at one in the very least.

As can be seen, even explaining, much less, defining Þéodisc Geléafa is a difficult task. Never the less, the reasons for being Theodish are much the same amongst all the theods. A need for a group identity is a very real need for most, if not all, human beings. Modern culture, and consequently its institutions do not always provide that. Theodish Belief attempts to.

Chapter II: History

Theodish Belief began with one man, Garman Lord. Garman was not alone in its early development, but if anyone can be said to be the founder of Theodism, he can. Others, such as Lord Æþelræd of Moody Hill Theod also contributed much while later folks like Swain and Eric Wódening did much to change the course of modern Theodism. The roots of Theodism are hard to trace. Leave it to say, it has roots in both Wicca and Germanic Heathenry. Garman began his path towards Theodish Belief as a Wiccan, studying in the Gardnerian tradition. In 1971, his coven made their High Priestess, the "Witch Queen." And as she was a "Queen," they also developed a council of advisors. Looking in a dictionary Garman found the term Witan (the Anglo-Saxon councils appointed by kings to advise them). Finding this word in a dictionary started Garman on a quest that would eventually lead to the foundation of Theodish Belief. In 1971, he and others founded the "The Coven Witan of Anglo-Saxon Wicca" (Garman Lord, "The Evolution of Þéodisc Belief: Part I" *Theod* Lammas, 1995).

The idea of Theodism did not truly begin to take form however, until July 4, 1976, when according to Garman Lord, the God and Goddess, Wóden (Odin) and Fríge (Frigga) appeared to him. Shortly thereafter, he founded the Witan Theod. In 1981, the Witan Theod became inactive, and Garman started publication of a magazine, Vikingstaff. This magazine created early

Theodish Belief's first contacts with the rest of Germanic Heathenry, which, at that time were only Ásatrúar. By 1985, the Witan Theod was active again, and it was at that time Garman Lord came up with the term Þéodisc Géleafa, "the belief of the tribe." By 1988, the Winland Ríce was founded. It consisted of two theods, Moody Hill Theod, a former Seax-Wicca coven and Géring Theod, the former Witan Theod. Garman Lord was sworn in as Lord Æþeling at Hallows of 1990. And, in 1991 at Midsummer, Garman hosted a gathering of over fifty Theodsmen. (Garman Lord, "The Evolution of Þéodisc Belief: Part II" *Theod* Lammas, 1995).

At that time, Theodism was still very basic, and still very much influenced by Wicca. Its rites were, for the most part, Wiccan, as were many of its beliefs. At this point however, some important developments took place. With the formation of the Winland Ríce, the *árung* of Æþeling was established (*árungas* had existed prior to this time, but not that of Æþeling). With it came the concepts of tribal luck (then expressed as the "king's luck), and the idea a leader of a theod had the gift of *ræd* (the idea the leader can receive divine guidance from the Gods). At that time, Theodish Belief focused on kingship, and even though there was no king, it was felt there would be one. Thus, most metaphysical concepts revolved around the idea of kingship. Other ideas such as the leadership needing the consent of the tribe, or the leader merely being a guardian of the tribal luck would not develop until later. It was in this period that Theodsmen performed the first Theodish blót. On Nov. 9, 1991, near where the Iroquois say the first werman (male) and woman appeared, in the State of New York, Garman Lord gave an animal to the Gods and Goddesses. At that time, Theodism was still giving the animal whole to the Gods and Goddesses much like the sacrifices of the ancient Hebrews in the Temple at Jerusalem. Later however, the idea would develop that such sacrifices must be eaten and shared between Gods and men (more like a sacred barbecue).

Gert McQueen, who would be influential in Theodism's development became a thrall of Moody Hill in 1989 after having met Garman Lord at a party. Moody Hill soon developed problems with Gert, and later Garman. By Hallows of 1991, a struggle began between the two theods, with the end result of both theods going their own ways in September of 1992. Despite the two groups separating, both still referred to what they did as Theodish. The number of Theodsmen fell dramatically after that from over fifty to nearly zero. Géring Theod did not cease to be active however. Gert was appointed to the Rede of the Ring of Troth (now the Troth), and both her and Garman began to publish articles in its magazine Idunna, as well as the Heathen magazine Mountain Thunder. Moody Hill had its own publishing ventures as well.

It was at this time Gert became aware of two other Anglo-Saxon Heathens. The brothers Eric and Swain Wódening had been publishing articles in Idunna. The Wódenings, unlike Garman had not come from a Wiccan background. Instead, after being raised Methodist, and then be-coming agnostics, they found their way to a brand of Anglo-Saxon Heathenry they had created themselves. They were aware of Wicca, and dismissed it out of hand, but an interest in Vikings, the runes, and the Dark Ages, lead them to Norse mythology. This in turn lead them to the fact their own English ancestors worshipped the same Gods. In seclusion, they developed their own religious rituals and beliefs. In time, they became aware of Ásatrú, but by the time they decided to join the AFA it was already defunct.

When in 1989, Swain learned of the Ring of Troth, they promptly joined, and soon after were writing articles. Their first full length articles were in the only Idunna published in 1991. By late 1992, Gert and the brothers Wódening were corresponding with each other, and by August of 1993, they were members of the Winland Ríce, and founders of Wednesbury Theod.

Not long after, the Winland Ríce began a new publishing venture with a booklet by Swain, Beyond Good and Evil. It saw publication along with the launch of THEOD Magazine in February of 1994. Up until then Swain and his brother both had been rather prolific contributors to the Troth's Idunna (13 articles in 1993 alone), but had not attempted any publication of their Heathen works outside of its pages. The Wódenings brought to Theodism the blót outline many theods use today. They also introduced symbel, a rite known to Ásatrúar, but one for which Theodsmen would become known. With Beyond Good and Evil, the Wódenings gave the concept of Wyrd, which Theodsmen were already familiar with, deeper meaning, and introduced the concept of *orlæg* (the idea that wrongs must be compensated for with restitution). Other metaphysical concepts were also introduced at that time, such as the idea of the tribe as an enclosure or innangarð, the difference between the sacred and the holy, and ideas on good and evil. They also elaborated on the idea of "worthing," the thought that a Heathen must be constantly striving to improve his or her self. Some of the ideas the Wódenings had borrowed from authors such as Edred Thorsson, others were the results of their own research.

Others soon began to join the Ríce, and Theodish Belief once again began to grow. In May of 1994, Swain hosted the only gathering ever co-sponsored by the Troth and a Theodish organization, Walburges 1994, which, for a several years, remained the largest Heathen gathering, held in the Midwest. The Ríce continued to grow during the years of 1994 and 1995, but there seemed to be incessant fighting with various Ásatrú organizations. In part, this was because of a continuation of the "Troth Wars" (a power struggle inside the Ring of Troth in 1994 and 1995). A good deal of it however, was due to paranoia on the Winland Ríce's part. Nonetheless, the Wednesbury King's School was founded as the first organized attempt at educating Theodsmen in 1994. In its day, it was thought to rival the Troth's Elder program, and many programs created since have used its structure as a basis. Also at this time, Eric Wódening and Winifred Hodge produced the first research on the concept of frið or frith, the peace and prosperity of the tribe that must be maintained at all costs.

In 1994, the Fresena Rike was founded with Gerd Groenwald as its leader. It was the first Theodish group to become independent of the Winland Ríce (in 1999) and survive. It perhaps, more than any other theod, sparked the movement towards true authenticity. The Fresena Rike was the first non-Anglo-Saxon theod, and it introduced such scholarly au-thors as Georges Dumezil and Mircia Eliada to Theodish Belief. This influx of new scholarly material had an impact on the intellectual development of Theodism. Finally, it was the first to produce sung liturgy in great quantity. While others had produced prayers in the old tongues, many in the form of songs, only the Fresena Rike did so with consistency. The Rike lapsed into a period of no activity a few years later but was revived as Axenthof Thiad in 2005. At one time, its numbers rivaled that of the Winland Ríce, and its members were known for their scholarship, liturgy, abilities with the ancient languages, and crafts.

At Midsummer in 1995, Garman was raised to *cyning* (king) of the Winland Ríce. This had immediate repercussions, good and bad. Two Theodsmen left shortly after for reasons debated to this day. Not long after another was outlawed when one of his thegns had a vision showing him as king. Yet, many things were accomplished that furthered Theodish Belief. From 1995 to 2000, the Winland Ríce continued to publish THEOD Magazine, Eric Wódening released We are Our Deeds (which addressed many of the ideas covered by Swain in Beyond Good and Evil in more depth), Garman published several booklets, and its numbers continued to grow. During this time the Winland Ríce, continued working on many of the things it had started in 1994. Bedes or prayers were composed in Old English and sung to harp accompaniment. A working liturgy was developed, while old Wiccan based rituals were dropped in favor of Heathen ones. Anglo-Saxon charms such as the Síð Galdor were reworked for use in modern ritual. Theodish ritual perhaps saw more change from 1994 to 1996 than it had in years.

By late 1995, Swain had grown tired of the constant fighting with other Heathens and Heathen organizations. Further, the outlawry of one of his former thegns deeply disturbed him. He asked to be released of his hold oath in early 1996. With no results to be seen on his request, he began to speak with Winifred Hodge and three other former members of the Ríce. The plan being discussed was to form a more democratic, more authentic Theodish organization. He and Winifred Hodge officially founded the Angelseaxisce Ealdriht on Midsummer of 1996 with the plighting of oaths.

The Angelseaxisce Ealdriht grew to become the largest Theodish organization ever. Unlike the Winland Ríce, it was more democratic, more scholarly, and unfortunately, often less organized. Instead of staying truer to authenticity however, it strayed just as far as the Winland Ríce had in other directions. Nevertheless, it did contribute a great deal to the evolution of Theodism. While the Winland Ríce remained relatively unchanged from 1997 until 2000, the Ealdriht was constantly reinventing its self. It did not make many innovations, but it did establish there were other forms of oaths than hold oaths, alternate means to entering Theodism than thralldom, and strengthened the idea of the tribal assembly. In addition, it perfected the rite of húsel, blót as a sacred feast.

Theodism continued to grow as other Theodish groups were founded. In September of 1999, the Green Thorn Grove was formed. It was dedicated to the study and practice of the ways of the Old Saxons and Anglo-Saxons. In June of 2000, members of Green Thorn Grove founded Vorstead Kindred to replace it. In December of 2000, after merging with another kindred, Vorstead became the Folk River Shire. By August 2002 (having become formally Theodish earlier that year) Folk River entered into fosterage under Garman *Cyning* of the Winland Ríce. This fosterage ended badly as by March 2003, Folk River Theod found its self in conflict with Gering Theod. Êrmund was elected war king (as the ancient Saxons only had kings in times of war) in order to deal with this conflict. This conflict ended in June of 2003 when Folk River broke all ties with Gering Theod. In Novemeber 2002, Folk River renamed its self Folcaha Sahsam Thiod, and took its present name of Sahsisk Thiod in September of 2004. Sahsisk Thiod expanded on ideas of kingship by raising the first war king, something that had not been done before. In addition, in being authentic to the ancient Saxon social structure, they paved the way for other tribal confederations. This made it possible for people to found teods resurrecting the ways of the Alamanni, Winnili, Quadi, and Turingii, and other ancient tribes using the tribal confederation model if they wished. Finally, Sahsisk Thiod was the first not to require hold oaths for ceorls (the lowest non-novice *árung* in most theods). Sahsisk Thiod took this bold step as a way of breaking away from the warband structure of many theods, and becoming more authentically a tribe. This was something that had been discussed in various theods since 1993, but never done. Up until then it was felt the "web of oaths" was necessary to bind a theod together.

In 2004, the Witan of the Ealdriht decided its goals were accomplished, and it split into the more authentic Theodish organizations of New Anglia and the Miercinga Theod. The move then was to encourage regionalism (the idea that tribes must be made up of folk living relatively close together), and towards more authentic reconstruction of ancient tribalism. It was New Anglia, based on discussions within the Ealdriht prior to its dissolution, that innovated more humane ways of sacrificing swine by using a knife as opposed to a sword (slitting the throat as opposed to chopping off the head). In addition, they were the first to make extensive use of god posts, although both the Fresena Rike and Wednesbury Theod had used them prior. New Anglia along with the Miercinga Theod revived the idea of burning grain for the dead in ancestral rites. These minor innovations when put together have a much greater impact on Theodism than would first appear. It shows a greater devotion to authenticity, as well as spirituality in worship.

Chapter III: A Case for Tribalism

In the history of Mankind, nearly every government or institution resembling a government has eventually failed. No governmental form has seemed capable of lasting more than a few hundred years, with only a few exceptions. Democracy with all its touted values has failed to be stable. Even governmental forms that have lasted thousands of years such as that of the Egyptian pharaohs eventually failed. Indeed, the only human social structure that has lasted is that of the tribe. Tribes have existed for as long as there has been written history. Of course, the cultures that recorded the tribes portray them as barbarians, as being somehow inferior (despite the fact the tribal society may be more technologically advanced in some aspects). As long as a people remained tribal, barring conquest, famine, or epidemic, they survived. Tribalism is perhaps the longest lasting, perhaps most stable social institution envisioned by Man.

There are many definitions of what a tribe is. The most basic is, "a people." Another basic one might be, "a tribe is a community of individuals." A dictionary definition is, "Any aggregate of people united by ties of descent from a common ancestor, community of customs and traditions, adherence to the same leaders, etc. (Random House Webster's College Dictionary, Random House, New York 1997). All of these definitions have one common element, people or the folk. In order for individuals to form a people or a folk, a tribe, it requires that something unite them. There are no tribes of one. Further, there must be reasons that they unite in such a way to form a tribe.

Tribalism, unlike most forms of social order and governance is almost instinctive. The other great apes also form similar social orders. Chimpanzees organize themselves into communities. These communities are 40 individuals or larger (depending on the area), and break down into smaller groups of up to six that travel together. The social order is one of hierarchy. The males order themselves in degrees of influence or power within the community with one male as the alpha. Gorillas have a similar social order. There is the silverback, one mature male that serves as the alpha. A troop's size ranges from 2 to 35 individuals. Generally, only the alpha male mates. Gibbons do not group in large groups, but in families with the parents and the children. Orangutans are about the only species of apes, which do not sort themselves into a family or near tribal structure. There, the males are solitary while the females head small family groups. Other primates such as the baboon also organize themselves into groups. For the baboon, this means males and females in one group with an alpha male. Overall, their social organization is not much different from chimpanzees.

Now, most will look at this, and say, "We have evolved far beyond the other primates." However, consider, can you survive in the wild? If you go by who has better chances of surviving in the wild, using only the resources available, the other primates, much less the other great apes, are as advanced, if not more so than we are. This is perhaps why other social structures fail. In the long run, they do not address the one key need of all humans, the need to survive. Other social structures than the tribe may address prosperity of all for a while, but eventually the wealth lands in the hands of a few. Non-tribal societies may address security for a while, but again, even that may fail as the privileged cease to care about the safety of the common man. Only the tribe has seemed to thrive as a social structure for Man on this planet. Although its social structure may differ from people to people, one essential element remains. That essential element is the family as a base unit.

The most basic unit of the tribe is the family. According to scholar Edward Goldsmith in his work, The Stable Society, the family is perhaps the earliest social organization in the history of Man (The Stable Society, The Wadebridge Press, 1978). The family in some form is nearly universal amongst humans save for a few exceptions. Even in societies where the family plays a less important role, it still exists, at least to nurture the young at their earliest ages. One can see the advantages of a strong family, even in modern society, where its position has been compromised. Perhaps, because the position of the family has been degraded, modern society is best at showing what happens when people have no family. Persons without families or having grown up without a family are more likely to have mental illnesses, commit suicide, commit violent crimes, or fall into the trap of addictions (not limited to drugs, alcohol, and sex addictions).

Also nearly universal according to Goldsmith, is the community, a group of families living together. This community may be divided into clans (which are extended families as a larger unit), the family, and community. Clans then make up the tribe (ibid). This is the most basic social structure of Mankind. Families form the basis for human social order. However, families do not always survive on their own, and there is a need to marry outside the family. Therefore, communities form. If these communities grow large, clans form as another unit, between the community and the family. If the community grows large enough, tribes form (communities united together).

Not a few scholars feel that society disintegrates without a social structure such as this. Durkheim felt that modern nation states are unstable because they fail to recognize the need for there to be an organized hierarchy of groups and subgroups. Further, he felt society could only be built from smaller groups amongst whom there were effective bonds. And, this was necessary for the well being of individuals, not just society at large (Emile Durkheim, "The solidarity of occupational groups". Talcott Parsons (ed.), Theories of Society, The Free Press, New York,1970).

Tribalism, because its basis lies ultimately in the family, addresses the issues of the society and the individual. In societies that still have strong family bonds, you do not see the crime, drug abuse, or suicide rates of those without. As a society loses family bonds its crime rate rises. This is reflected in the United States own history. According to the United States Department of Health and Human Services, girls without a father are two and a half times likely to get pregnant, while boys without fathers are 63 per cent more likely to run away and 37 per cent more likely to use drugs. (U.S. Department of Health and Human Services, National Center for Health Statistics, Survey on Child Health, Washington, DC, 1993). In a study done in New Orleans hospitals, 80 percent of children admitted as psychiatric patients had no fathers. In another study, children with emotional support from a family as opposed to the structure provided by a teacher had fewer behavioral problems (NICHD, Child Development Vol. 74, Number 6. November/December, 2003). Another study linked the rise in crime to the rise in out of wedlock births from 1974 to 1995 (Mackey and Coney, "Human Sex Ratios as a Function of the Woman's Psychodynamics – a Preliminary Study," Ethology and Sociobiology, 8, 49-60). The family is not an option for a society, but a necessity. Without the family, all social order starts to unravel. Therefore, any social structure that does not encourage the family or use it as the basis for its structure is bound for failure. Modern republics such as the United States place emphasis on the individual, and a rise in crime, mental illness, and drug reflects that overemphasis on the individual. Communism saw a similar result, as does half a dozen other forms of social order that do not involve the family.

Beyond the family, the tribe better addresses the needs of the community. Because tribes tend to be local, the very people involved make decisions on local issues. Some national government far away with no real involvement does not decide on them. How many times, has Congress decided to place a dam where it is not wanted? How many times have state legislatures placed prisons where a community does not want them, but ignores those that do desire them? Modern government, with all its commotion about protecting human rights, is in reality, very impersonal. That is not to say the nation state is a failure. It is to say that perhaps a nation state should be composed of tribes. The current subdivisions of the federal and state governments of the

United States are irrelevant to the needs of the local people. Every eight or so years, areas are "redistricted" according to the needs of the Constitution, a peace of paper that was intended to look out for the needs of the people, but has been compromised. Even when it was not compromised, its criteria for its Congressional districts were based on population, not community. The smallest unit the Constitution addressed was the state. Sadly, today's mobility of individuals caused by corporate America (managerialism at its finest), would prevent tribes from forming in any form naturally, be it the tribes of old, or the farming communities of one hundred years ago.

Theodish Belief therefore attempts to form tribes intentionally. These tribes are not political in nature; they would still exist within the nation state. However, the hopes are that Þéodisc Geléafa can bring back the benefits of the closeness of community the tribe provided. By encouraging a natural social order based on families, and other units of social organization with personal bonds, the pitfalls of a modern society with weak familial bonds can be avoided. The basis for Theodish Belief is the *mægð* , the *sibb* , the *dryht* , and the gild. The *mægð* is the modern nuclear family. The *sibb* is the extended family. The *dryht* would have been a warband in the days of old, its individual bonded together by hold oaths. Today it is more like a martial arts dojo (albeit with religious practices as well), its members practicing both ancient and modern European martial arts, and worshipping together. A gild is like a *dryht* in that its members are bonded together for hold oaths, but it is formed for other purposes such as practicing a craft or profession. Both the *dryht* and the gild are seen as artificial families or brotherhoods. The theod or þéod would be the union of these social units. All have a common cultural identity, common history, as well as shared customs, traditions, and religion. It is these things that unite them into a theod, and helps them to reap the benefits of the unity of a tribe. To form an even closer bond, many theods of Theodish Belief use what is called the web of oaths. Every person is connected to some one else either through a hold oath or by blood or adoption with these oaths accumulating at its apex in the leader of the tribe.

Chapter IV: Reviving Ancient Tribes

At first the idea of a reviving an ancient tribe may seem ludicrous. After all, if a tribe is to be held together by a common identity, a shared history, and shared tradition; it would make more sense to find people with those things in common. Unfortunately, modern society is so diverse that it is near impossible to find those with such things in common. Further, because most of us are coming from a Christian background, our shared history is a less than desirable thing. Finally, there is the matter of consistency. One could take bits and pieces of the lore (the information that survived down to us about ancient Germanic religion in the form of Anglo-Saxon poems, the Eddas, Roman accounts, and other accounts by outsiders, and numerous other texts), from various Germanic peoples, and construct a modern tribe on this. The problem is that it may not be consistent. Just because, the Norse and Anglo-Saxons spoke similar languages, and the same cultural tree spawned both, does not mean their cultures were one, and the same. And, unfortunately for us, these differences may not be apparent on the surface, but would necessitate an in depth study of the cultures. In some cases, there may even be conflicts of beliefs particularly in the area of social structure or the position of women (women in Anglo-Saxon culture held the highest position of any culture at the time in Europe).

As said previously in this book, one could start new Heathen tribes, and perhaps still enjoy the benefits of tribalism. However, as also been said, it would take a great deal of work in establishing a social structure, creating customs and tradition, not to mention getting into issues of establishing identity. These would be disadvantages, which one may not have when reviving an ancient tribe. With a new tribe made from scratch, one would not have an established history to look back on, at least not for many years, nor would one necessarily have tribal ancestors. A history held in common by all members is a   crucial element in tribal society, while tribal ancestors played a great role in ancient Germanic religion. It could be argued, that reviving an ancient tribe would have the same problems. However, there at least, an attempt is being made to reconnect to a history and ancestry. With a new tribe, that cannot be done as a common history does not yet exist, and a common ancestry may not be acknowledged even if it exists.

There are other reasons however, that reviving an ancient tribe may be preferable. Pure, true Heathenry has not existed for nearly nine hundred years. Since then the Germanic languages and other things such as art, the very expressions of human existence, have changed to suit the new religion. They no longer reflect Heathen beliefs, thoughts, or ideas. A culture's beliefs are expressed in more than sentences and phrases. Single words contain meanings reflecting the attitudes of the culture. Artwork too reflects these things. For example, the common translation of Wyrd is "fate" although sometimes it is also translated "providence"), a concept it has very little relation to. These translations may well apply to later Anglo-Saxon texts after Christian beliefs had been accepted at least by the learned. However, we know from older beliefs that Wyrd was more akin to karma, than any unchanging fate or the will of the Ése (Æsir) and Wen (Vanir). This example is one that is more apparent to modern Heathens, however, there are numerous others that may not so. It is these symbols one seek when looking to reconstruct the beliefs of the tribe.

The Whorf Hypothesis states that language determines how a person thinks, and that the culture shapes language and hence language reflects the culture's beliefs. Further, not only does language give ideas words, but it also shapes the ideas. That is, what one thinks is determined by their language (what Whorf referred to as linguistic determinism). In essence, culture shaped language and language shaped culture (John B. Carroll (ed.), Selected Writings of Benjamin Lee Whorf Cambridge: MIT Press, 1956). Similarly, many say the same of art, that culture creates art, and art shapes culture. One could probably take nearly every aspect of human life and see how it somehow shapes the cultures we live in. Hence, in order to get completely in touch with the religion of an ancient tribe, one would have to learn about its art forms, language, even study their history, in addition to customs, traditions, and rites.

Going back to the idea that the Norse culture was not exactly the same as the Anglo-Saxon (indeed there were differences between the Angles, Saxons, and Jutes), one cannot take a hodgepodge approach and be consistent due to the fact things can be easily missed if one is not looking at the "whole picture." If one, say only looks at the Icelandic sagas and Eddas to try to recreate a Norse theod, they may miss the central ideas behind ancient Norse Heathenry. Indeed, in order to make sure they know the central ideas, they must study not only the surviving written record, but also Old

Norse (for ideas lie behind the words of its language), its art forms (for religious expression is often found in art), and anything else that might relate to Old Norse culture. One cannot take a mishmash approach and hope to achieve anything. One cannot afford to pick and choose.

Now, to a degree one must use a mix of the various Germanic cultures, as there are many gaps in our knowledge of ancient Heathenry. The Anglo-Saxon corpus contains information not seen in the Norse accounts that are helpful to the Norse practitioner nonetheless, and vice versa, (the same is true of information left on the Frisian, Gothic, and all the Germanic cultures). However, these gaps generally fall in the rather conservative area of religious ritual (where not much may have changed since the age of proto-Germanic culture). In other areas such as social customs, we have much more information, and it is there, there are likely to be problems. For sake of consistency alone, using the customs, traditions, and to a small extant, written law of one ancient tribe makes more sense.

Consistency is very important especially since reviving an ancient tribe takes much study, and cannot be gone into lightly. One must acquire the necessary academic works, and learn the scholarly opinions on the accepted views of academia on the tribe. One must also become acquainted with Christian bias; even in modern works (translators often insert Christian bias into translations of poems where there is none for example). It is a long process and can take years to complete.

For that first step one must choose which tribe one wishes to revive, and whether or not there is sufficient information to do so. If there is not enough surviving lore, one may be better off founding a new tribe, or reviving another ancient tribe. After all, the benefits of reviving an ancient tribe are lost if there is not enough information about the social structure, and at least some of the beliefs and practices of the tribe. The factors for choosing a tribe are best left to the individual. Some of these factors may be, but are not limited to one's ancestry, language, the culture they live in, ideas on religious practices, or Gods and Goddesses one is closest to. One must keep in mind during the process they are not so much reviving an ancient tribe, as founding a new one based on the ancient tribe's principles. There will be, and must be differences between the ancient tribe and the modern due to gaps in information, changes in our host society, and simply that we are not the ancient Heathens.

The second step in reviving an ancient tribe is scholarly study. This requires obtaining many works on the tribe, and figuring out exactly what scholars feel the tribe was like. One will want to look at several areas, none being more important than the others are. Social structure, religious practices, customs and traditions, folklore, all play a role in a tribe's culture. Therefore, study cannot be limited to one area. One will want to read books from the fields of history, mythology, folklore, religious studies, anthropology, sociology, and archaeology. As these tribes no longer exist, history and archaeology may be the most important and available, but when other resources exist, one must look at them. One should always check a book's validity. What are the author's credentials? What reviews have been done of the book by known authorities? Do other books express the same general ideas? If a book is unique in its outlook, the author seems to have no field of expertise even close to what the book is about, makes far out undocumented claims, and in reviews, it is noted for its basing its ideas in less than known fact, it might be a good idea not to use the book for source material. One good way to tell if a book may be worthwhile is to look and see if it is foot or end noted. Foot and end noting shows the scholar writing the book is attempting to document where they got their ideas. The other thing to look for is the bibliography. If the bibliography contains well known academic works by noted authors, and many of them, the book may be worthwhile.

Once one has done enough academic study to know the tribe they are wishing to reconstruct, they can set about designing the tribe. Most things, if one has done their study will already be done for them. The social structure for example of many ancient Germanic structures is known, or can be surmised from surviving materials. Law codes, while Christian often give clues to ancient Heathen custom, while many Church documents forbidding pagan practices can give more clues. The primary areas one will want to focus on (at fist anyway) are social structure, custom and tradition, and religious practices. One cannot be too detailed in their studies of a tribe. Failures in Theodish Belief in the past happened because not enough detail was sought in researching the culture of the relevant ancient tribes. Theodsmen were happy with just a superficial appearance of the ancient theod with little to no real relevance to the ancient tribe. This made the theods look more like role playing communities than anything resembling a tribe or even a religious congregation.

One must keep in mind they are trying to develop the following things, a common identity, a common history, shared customs and traditions as well as a common ancestry. These things make a tribe. Common history is at first easy, and then hard at the same time. One's early history is that of the ancient tribe, the deeds of the ancestors and adopted ancestors one will look back on for boasts in symbel. However, history is never frozen in time, and with time, a theod will develop a modern history as well, and this cannot be ignored either. For folks to share in this history, they must be active and involved in the theod. Otherwise, they will not be a part of that history, and consequently not truly a part of the tribe. In time, members of the theod will be remembered in symbel as generations pass. Our present will become history. Those that have done little or nothing will fall outside the bounds of this history, and it will be as if they were never a part of the tribe at all. As they never became a part of the common identity, they will not be a part of the common history.

Developing a common identity is something that can only come with time through interaction of the tribe. People must worship together, share the same ideas, practice the same rites, and interact with each other a great deal. To no small degree this means involvement with each other's personal lives, the sharing of hopes and dreams, the sharing of triumphs and failures. It also means folks must work towards the common good of the tribe. Every deed, somehow, even if it ultimately benefits one's self, must help the tribe. It also means there is little room for conflicting interests in one's life. One's spouse and family comes first, and then the tribe. While important, the individual is secondary to those that depend on him or her. To a great amount, shared customs and traditions reinforce this shared tribal identity.

Shared traditions and customs work a long way to creating a common history and identity. It is these things, we do from year to year that help bond the tribe together as much as anything. A tradition may be anything from using a wreath to swear oaths on at Yule to the songs used at funerals to the hold oaths a tribe uses. Traditions and customs are the things a tribe has in common that largely make them a tribe. They cover a wide variety of things from the thews or virtues of the tribe to how one performs a rite. It can take a lifetime for a theod to develop customs and traditions, and that process never truly ends.

As to common ancestry, this may not seem important. However, one qualifier for being a tribe is common descent from some ancestor. For many people of Germanic descent this is not a problem. According to Taticus, the Germanic tribes traced their descent back to the sons of Mannus. This descent is as valid now as it was 2,000 years ago. For those of non-Germanic descent, adoption is as valid a way to this legacy as birth as any. The legends surrounding Mannus are lost, but a similar figure exists in Hindi beliefs, Manu. In Vedic texts, Manu is the first man and seen as the father of many royal dynasties (Yama, a being separate from Manu is given as the first man in other Vedic texts, showing how diverse ancient beliefs can be). Some scholars feel his name may be cognate to the word "man." Mannus therefore, may be seen as a father of "peoples," a legendary figure dating from the time of the Indo-Europeans, and nearly everyone of Germanic descent can trace their lines back to him. The point is regardless of biological descent, any member of a theod can trace common descent from an ancestor (although that ancestor may be very ancient). Ancient genealogies were, after all, in many cases semi-mythical.

All of these things go beyond just establishing things a tribe shares to be a tribe. What they ultimately do is bring the *dóm* (Old English for "law, judgment, ordeal, reputation," used here to mean "tribal wyrd"), or "tribal" *orlæg* of the ancient tribe back into being. That is, just as Norsemen in the sagas were said to inherit the örlög of their ancestors, so too, if everything is done right, the modern tribe receives the *dóm* of the ancient tribe. In doing so, the new or modern theod, will have built its self upon ancient precedent, and hopefully receive whatever *mægen* or "spiritual might" the ancient tribe had. Just as in symbel, one's *gielp* (boast of ancestry and past deeds) is intended to establish a precedent on which one can base their *béot* (vow to do something) they are about to make, the process of reviving a tribe calls up the precedents of the ancient tribe for that which the new tribe is about to do. The new theod is not the old tribe re-born, but a descendant. A descendant, which like the ancient Norseman receives the of their ancestors. As yet, perhaps no theod has ever achieved that level of being. It is perhaps something that only future generations will see. When it does happen, then we will have truly reconnected with the ancient Heathen tribesman, their ways, their worldview.

Again, the outline of Learning, Enacting, and Becoming given in Chapter I applies. With the first step, one is learning about the tribe they are seeking to revive, with the second step, one is putting what one

learned into action, and with the third, one is trying to reconnect to the ancient tribe in order to inherit its *dóm*
. One can almost view this as a ritual action; the result being one of connecting with the ancient tribe. All academic study and deeds aside however, a new theod's rituals determine as much as anything whether they will reconnect with their ancient ancestors. It also requires ritual action in the form of ancestor worship, symbel, and fainings for the Gods and Goddesses. It means performing rituals very similar to what the ancient tribe might have done. The ancient Heathens felt that they could rewrite Wyrd to a small degree through the spoken word, and this is what a modern theod tries to do with its rites. They fain the Gods and Goddesses for inspiration and guidance, they boast the ancestors in symbel, and worship them that they may be more like them. Not every rite will be towards reviving the ancient culture, many, by necessity must be geared towards today's needs. However, a good number should be. And to be truthful, this is not something the ancient Heathens with their ancestor worship, deep respect for the dead that have went before them would be unfamiliar with.

There is much beyond this academic research and enacting with deed, word, and rite. Ultimately, the folk make up the tribe. Even if one has done flawless research, has every scrap of lore on a tribe, and created a working cultural system others die for, it means little if one has no folk. There are no theods of one. This of course means one must garner interest in the theod. If two or three formed the theod or more people this is not a problem. However, if one great visionary did it, then you may have a problem. You must attract folk to your theod, and this may be more difficult than everything else you have done.

Chapter V: Law and Virtue

Laws and virtues are one area one cannot be specific about in Theodish Belief as these things will vary from theod to theod. Largely, this is because too many confuse the different aspects of law. Many things were true of all Germanic tribes. Many things were true of only one or two tribes. Once can say all of the Germanic peoples practiced blót. One cannot say that all practiced blót in the way portrayed in the *Heimskringla* by Snorri Sturluson. One can say that all of the tribes worshipped in groves. One cannot say that they all worshipped in oak groves at the height of Walpurgis. Therefore, when speaking of laws and virtues, one must tread very carefully when speaking of commonalities amongst the modern theods of Theodish Belief.

Most in Germanic Heathenry will have probably heard the word thew or thews applied when referring to what Theodsmen do, whether it be "law" or "custom." This is an incorrect usage even though all Theodsmen have probably used thew as such, on occasion. Thews in the least are the traditions and customs of a tribe. At the most, thews are the virtues a tribe holds highest. Thew is not law however. In truth, there are many different forms of "law" in Theodism, and all of them handled differently. Therefore, to understand Theodish custom and law, one must first understand the terms.

Æ is an Old English word for law (with the cognates Old Saxon *éo*, Old Frisian *á* or *éwa*, "law"; Old Norse *ei* or *ey* "ever") that would best describe universal law. Æ is the first layer laid down by Wyrd, and is unchanging due to the number of precedents upholding it. The word is related to words meaning "eternal" or ever lasting (such as Old English *Æfre* "ever" and *á* "always, forever"). In Old English, the idea of it being the "law of the universe" was strong enough that the Christian converts used it of "God's Law." When we speak of commonalities in tradition or custom of the theods, we are probably speaking of *Æ*. *Æ* dictates that we worship the Gods, it dictates that if I get an cut and do not take care of it, it gets infected. *Æ* dictates that the Law of Relativity works. *Æ* governed things that for the ancient Germanic Heathen were universal.

A second form of law is that of tribal law, or *dóm*. *Dóm* is the law created by the tribe through their deeds as a tribe. More specifically, it refers to the judgments in the tribal things and moots (note, that it can also be used of the tribal "wyrd"). Once, these judgments become customary, they may be referred to as *lagu* or law (though *dóm* may also be used). *Dóm* ultimately derives from the same root as "to do," and is related to the word "deeds" and is the Old English version of our word "doom." It derived from the Indo-European base of *dhe "to put, place do, make" (it has cognates in Sanskrit dhaman- "law," and Greek. themis "law"). Thus, *dóm* or doom is something that has been done. And, deeds that are done are recorded in the Well of Wyrd, and therefore form one of its layers. Layers in the Well of Wyrd, symbolic of the past, come bubbling back to the surface to influence the present represented by the World Tree. *Dóm* can be thought of as intentional, tribal karma. It is intentional in it is determined by the tribal leaders and moots. It is karma, in the idea it works on the principles of Wyrd.

Lagu derives from proto-Germanic *lagan "to put, lay." It is seen in the term , cognate to Old Norse, örlög a term used to refer to one's personal wyrd. Lagu is the layers of deeds laid in the Well of Wyrd by the tribe (if you are new to all of this, it will be understandable after reading Chapter VI). It operates on the same idea as Wyrd its self, that deeds one does determines the deeds of the future. The deeds of the tribe in assembly are laid down as layers of water or "recorded," in the Well of Wyrd, where they come bubbling back up from the bottom of the Well or "the past" to the top of the Well to be poured on the World Tree by the Norns or "the Present."

Ancient Germanic law worked on the idea of precedent, what the tribe had ruled before is what was to be done again. Unless, someone could expend sufficient strength to set a new precedent, it was these precedents, the law, that determined how any case brought before a thing would be handled. Occasionally, a king or folkmoot would decide that the laws needed to be changed, and they would do so. Even then, it was the deeds of the tribe (in formal setting), that determined the law. Modern Common Law works on the same principles.

Another form of law created by the tribe is *sidu* or custom. *Sidas* are the traditions of the tribe and may be anything from the way a tribe conducts a rite to the idea that one only eats ham on Yule. A custom of a tribe can also be referred to as a *þéaw* or thew. However, sidu is the stronger of the two terms. A habit can be called a *þéaw*, but only something as significant as say dancing the Maypole at Sumerdæg would be thought a *sidu*. Some may see the concept of *sidu*, as unimportant compared to the importance modern society places on written law. In truth, custom and tradition have guided Mankind far longer. When ancient China was suffering incessant warfare, it had plenty of laws, many of them written. It took Confucius writing down the customs of the Chinese in the form of maxims for the situation to change. Custom can dictate how one treats a guest, what one does prior to a rite to the Ése (Æsir), or what things a bride and groom can do on the day of their wedding. Some customs are associated with superstitions one cannot readily explain, others may have a basis in common sense. Regardless, customs work to control human behavior. Tradition (which I have used interchangeably with custom when I shouldn't) is no different, except in that it is more formal. (I am indebted to Êrmund Alderman and his article at: http://sahsisk.org/thiodisk_law.htm for much of this discussion).

Laws, customs, traditions are all things that help give a theod structure. In ancient times, much like at the Icelandic Althing of the Middle Ages, someone that had to memorize the laws of the tribe probably recited them each year. No doubt, there were experts in the law. Those laws that were common sense, unlike today's states may not have even been considered a part of the law, but fell under the heading of sidu. In the old law codes we rarely see laws outlawing murder, instead we see the consequences that happen to someone that does. Æ played an important role here in that all knew it was wrong to steal, kill, maim, rape, lie....

Consequently, when discussing what Theodish Belief holds to be the highest "thews" we must only discuss Æ. We must discuss only the things that all ancient Germanic tribes held to be law. Even then, we must discuss it in the most general of ways. There are many things that each theod does differently or handles differently. In general, all theods have the following in common:

a) Worship of the Germanic Gods: All theods worship the Germanic gods. They may not have all the same gods (for example one group may worship Éostre, another may not), but what deities they do worship are of the Germanic pantheon nonetheless.

    i) Worship: Most theods have some form of worship besides the sacrifice of animals. This may include libations, bedes or prayers, or gifts of items to the Gods and Goddesses.

    ii) Blót: All theods believe in the power of sharing meat with the Gods and Goddesses, and the making sacred of an animal to do so.

    iii) Symbel: All theods use the rite of symbel as a way of bonding the tribe together, and as a way of praising the Gods and Goddesses and the Idesa and Ýlfe (the ancestors).

b) Rites for Life Events: Each theod has rites for events in an individual's life that may or may not include the Gods and Goddesses.

    i) Birth Rites: Rites performed at the birth of a child.

    ii) Marriage: Rites performed to unite a werman and woman

    iii) Death Rites: Rites performed for those about to die or the newly dead.

c) Holy Tides: All theods have holy tides when the tribe gathers together to worship the Gods.

d) Sacral Leadership: All theods recognize some form of sacral leadership. All believe that certain leaders have sacral duties they must be held to. The ideas on sacral leadership vary, but are present in all theods.

e) Tribal Assemblies: All theods use some form of tribal assembly. That assembly may serve as a way to endorse the decisions of the leadership, or as a voting body with the power to over rule the leadership. In some cases, there may be a hierarchy of assemblies. How assemblies are handled varies a great deal amongst the theods.

f) Structured Society: All theods use some form of hierarchy in which certain "classes" perform certain jobs. Generally, all freemen are thought equal within a tribe, but there are those whose service has caused them to be listened to more closely. In some theods, the leadership acknowledges one's class or *árung* based on certain laws of advancement. In other theods, it is the folkmoots that determine one's *árung*. Regardless of how *árung* is determined, few theods would defy the folk determining who is at what level.

g) Metaphysical or Legal Concepts: There are several metaphysical or legal concepts every theod holds in common although the interpretation may vary.

     i) Frith: The idea, the tribe must maintain peace and prosperity within the tribe according to its own laws.

ii) Wyrd: The concept that our deeds determine what happens in the present and the future.

iii) Sacred Enclosures: All theods see the tribe as an enclosure, unique unto its self, and owing to no one else.

iv) Grith: The idea when interacting with other tribes, they maintain peaceful relations with each other, unless there is good reason otherwise.

v) Oaths: All theods maintain that oaths are sacred and should not be broken. How oaths are handled otherwise may differ from theod to theod.

vi) Restitution: One must make restitution for any wrong done, otherwise, they will suffer consequences in this world and the next. Exactly how restitution is handled will very from theod to theod.

vii) Family: All theods maintain that the family was an important fixture in all ancient Germanic tribes.

viii) Rights: Every theod has certain rights freemen are entitled to. These will vary from theod to theod, but basically, are there to ensure individuals are treated justly.

These are by no means all the things that the theods have in common. Doubtless, others have been overlooked. One perhaps is self-determination of a theod. Self-determination means that no one can define that theod, only its folk and leadership can. This is the very reason there is little detail to the above list. While all theods may believe in some form of the listed ideas, each will have its own interpretation. The idea that a theod could determine its own structure, beliefs, and customs runs contrary to the Theodism of ten years ago. The Theodism of ten years ago maintained that one detailed template would do for any theod. This was regardless of whether it drew inspiration from the ancient Goths, the ancient Angles, the ancient Franks, or any of the other Germanic tribes. This "one size fits all" approach could never produce true Theodism. The Goths' social structure differed within the greater cultural classification of Goth, much less, from say, the Varni, Saxons, or Thurungians. For there to be true Theodism in the sense that each tribe was unique to the customs and traditions of the ancient tribe it was reviving, requires there be differences. And, it is that idea that has produced the Theodism of today.

Chapter VI: Wyrd

To understand Theodism, one must first understand Wyrd. Most Heathens probably have a working understanding of the concept, but Theodish Belief takes that concept to new levels. Most modern Germanic Heathens have a good understanding of Wyrd as applied to individuals, perhaps even small groups of people. However, they never think about its implications when applied to larger groups. Therefore, a brief review of Wyrd is needed before getting into its deeper meanings. Wyrd is one of the most difficult concepts to explain in modern Heathenry; therefore saying that not every theod may view Wyrd as presented here must preface the following discussion.

Before discussing Wyrd its self we must state that Wyrd is not fatalistic in nature, nor is it existential in nature. One has free will to a degree to determine the outcome of their lives, but there are some absolutes that will affect that outcome. These we will address later when we talk about a person's *orlæg*. The word Wyrd is derived from Indo-European *wert- "to turn," and related to Old English weorþan "to become," and Latin vertere"to turn." Its orignal meaning therefore may have been "that which has turned" which shifted in meaning to "that which has become." Within the lore we see two models of Wyrd. One is the well and the tree, that is the well Urðarbrunnr and the tree Yggdrasil of Eddic myth. According to the Prose Edda:

Ask veit ek ausinn, Heitir Yggdrasil,
Hárr baðmr heilagr, Hvíta-auri;

Þaðan koma döggvar, Es í dala falla;
Stendr æ yfir gronn Urðarbrunni.

An ash I wit standing Called Yggdrasil,
A high holy tree Sprinkled with white clay,
Thence come the dews That in the dales fall;
Stands it always ever green Over Wyrd's Well.
(Gylfaginning 16, Prose Edda)

The well Urðarbrunnr is at the base of the tree,
and it is here that the Norns do their work.

Þaðan koma meyiar, margs vitandi,
þrár, ór þeim sæ, er und þolli strendr;
Urð héto eina, aðra Verðandi
--scáro scíði--, Skuld ina þriðio;
þær lög löumlgðo, þær líf kuro
alda bornom, *ørlög* (ON) seggia

Thence come the maidens, Mighty in wisdom,
Three from the place, Under the tree,
Wyrd is called one, Another Werðende
Scored they on wood, *Orlæg* is the third;
There Laws they laid, There life chose,
To men's sons, And spoke orlay (Völuspa 20-25)

It is with these activities that the three greater
Norns determine men's lives. Each action they do is
equated in some way with the determination of *orlæg* or
ørlög (ON). Scoring in wood can be seen as inscribing
runes, a magical act which is seen with curses and attempts to receive blessings. Scoring is one of the things
in the Havamal required if one is to learn the runes.

Chosing life is not so much a chosing of life as chosing of death. Wyrd is most often associated with death in Old English poetry, for death is the ultimate outcome of one's life. Finally, they speak *orlæg*, the "primal layer" that determines the course of men's lives. These actions represent that part of life, which is not determined by free will, those things we cannot change, or cannot change without great difficulty.

But Wyrd is not fatalistic in the sense of pre-destination. There is room for free will. This is represented by the interaction between the well and the tree. The well represents the past.

"The well is named for Urth; her name represents the 'past.' This past includes the actions of all beings who exist within the enclosing branches of Yggdrasil: men, gods, giants, elves, etc. Like the water, these actions find their way back into the collecting source; as happens, all actions become known, fixed, accomplished. In one sense, it is such actions that form the layers or strata that are daily laid in the well by the speaking of the *ørlög* (ON). The coming into the well is orderly and ordered; events are clearly related to each other, and there is pattern and structure in their storage." (Paul Bauschatz, *The Well and the Tree: World and Time in Early Germanic Culture*, Amherst: The University of Massachusetts Press, page 20)

The tree represents the present. Each day the Norns water the tree from the well bringing actions of the past back to influence the present represented by the tree.

Enn er þat sagt at nornir þær, er byggva við Urðarebrunn, taka jvern dag vatni brunninum ok með aurinn þann, er liggr um brunninn, ok ausa upp yfir askinn, till þess at eigi skulu limar hans trena eða funa, en þat vatn er sva heilagt, at allir hlutir, þeir er þar koma I brnninnn, verða sva hvitir sem henna su, er skjall heitir er innanliggr eggskurn.

Further it is said that these Norns who dwell by the Well of Wyrd, take water from the well everyday, and with it that clay above the well, and sprinkle it over the Ash, to the end that its limbs do not wither nor rot: for that water is so holy that all things which come there into the well become as white as an egg white(Gyfaginning 16, Prose Edda)

Thus Wyrd is cyclical in nature the past being brought into the present only to seep back into the past. The well and the tree was not the only model that represented Wyrd in the minds of the ancient Heathens. They also saw it as threads woven on a great loom. In the first lay of Helgi Hundingsbani in the Elder Edda, the Norns set up a loom in the sky anchoring the threads north, east, south, and west. It is implied that with this they weaved the life events of the child Helgi. Individuals are generally seen as simple threads within the loom instead of the entire web. Through out the lore, we see references to the thread of a man's life. While the well model shows the interaction of the past with present, the thread model shows the interconnectivity of life best. Each thread touches and impacts thousands of others. Within a theod, it is represented by a section of the web, all its threads touching one upon the other.

Wyrd changes, yet some parts of it are unchanging. An apt comparison might be our own universe. Everything must obey the laws of the universe as interpreted by science, but the events that take place due to those laws are not predetermined. Thus the Norns or *Wyrdæ* set down certain laws by which the events of men's lives, tribes, and the world must abide by, but the events themselves are determined for the most part by our own actions. This is known in the lore as *scyld* or skuld (ON). *Orlæg* is the third Norn and her name means "that which is obligated to become." These obligations are the things men cannot change. They are the things preordained by the *Wyrdæ* or the Gods or from an ancestor's karma to come to pass, and nothing we do can change it. The Old English word *orlæg* also meant "sin" something one was obligated to pay for.

Each person has their own personal "wyrd" or *orlæg*. Folklore and the Icelandic sagas demonstrate the absolutes of one's *orlæg*. Within the pages of Grimm's Teutonic Mythology, one can find several tales that illustrate this. At birth according to folklore, three Norns show up at one's birth. The first two generally bless the child, while the third issues a curse (Grimm, Jacob, Stallybrass (tr.), Teutonic Mythology, London: George Bell and Sons, 1900). Such a tale is found in Book VI of Saxo's Danish history. Fridleif takes his three year old son to the temple to pray to three maidens. The first two granted charm and generosity, but the third said he would be niggardly in the giving of gifts. This speaking of *orlæg* is of utmost importance to the life of the individual. While the individual may determine the events of their lives, the blessings or curses will determine the outcome of many of these events. The Gods and Goddesses too may determine one's *orlæg*. Perhaps the best illustration of this is the tale of Starkad. Starkad was brought before an assembly of the Gods. There, Odin and Thor alternately blessed and cursed him. Thor said he would be childless. Odin gave him three life spans. Thor said he would commit a foul deed in each life. Odin gave him the best in clothing and weapons. Thor stated he should never have land or estates. This went on until Thor and Odin were through cursing and blessing him, at which point the Gods ordained that all this shall happen to Starkad. The Gods thus in part set Starkad's *orlæg*.

In addition, to the speaking of *orlæg* at birth, and deemings of the Gods, inheritance of an ancestor's *orlæg* will impact one's life. The ancient Heathens felt that one could inherit parts of the soul of an ancestor. Such was the case with Olaf the Unholy (called Saint Olaf by Christians), whom they felt was thre reincarnation of an earlier Heathen King Olaf. Glumr in Viga Glum Saga claims to have the hamingja or luck of his grandfather.

All of these things plus one's own actions contribute to *orlæg*. Life is not totally pre-determined, nor is it totally ruled by free will. Some things are bound to happen, while others we can make happen.

Tribes like individuals have *orlæg*. This is probably best referred to as *dóm* as covered in Chapter V. It is the collective actions of the tribe laid down. It is their customs, their karma, their traditions and law. A tribe like an individual has a collective *orlæg*, determined by the Gods, the *Wyrdæ*, and the acts of its members as a whole and as individuals past and present. This *orlæg* is impacted by many things such as the deeds of the tribal members, its *mægen* or hamingja (ON) or luck, favor of the Gods and Goddesses, the deeds of its leaders. The tribe is a unit unto its self, like a clan, family or individual. It has *mægen* and *orlæg*. The purpose of many of its collective acts is to ensure that good *orlæg* continues. Its customs are performed because they have always brought *mægen* in the past. The laws exist to make sure no one harms the *mægen* of the tribe, and set a dangerous new *orlæg*. Each action one takes has a chance to set a new precedent for the tribe and one's self. A new precedent can mean that the results of any given action may change. Thus, a tribe that has always known victory in battle might know defeat as was the case with the Vandals and Lombards. The Lombards, then known as the Winni went to war with the Vandals. Out numbered and knowing Woden (Odin) had already promised victory to the Vandals turned to Frige (Frigga). She told them at dawn to face the east with their women, with the women's hair over their faces. She then turned Woden's bed to face the Lombards. When he awoke, he said, "Who are these longbeards?" Frige responded, "Now you have named them, you must give them victory." Ancient Germanic custom required one give a gift when naming, thus Woden owed the Lombards a gift. By turning to Frige, the Lombards used an old precedent, gifting for naming to set a new one, victory in battle.

Tribal *orlæg* is of utmost importance to the leaders of a theod as is its *mægen*. They can mean success or failure for the theod. Every action therefore is thought out carefully. Frith generally is maintained within the theod at all cost to prevent an *orlæg* of strife developing and destroying the theod. The Gods and

Goddesses are worshipped and gifted regularly to ensure their favor. All within the theod must keep to its goals. Individuals's actions affect the theod, and the *orlæg* of the theod affects them. The threads of each individual make up the theod's *orlæg*, and thus it is difficult some times in one's life to see where their own deeds caused an outcome, and where it was the theod's *orlæg* that caused it. Just as theods have their own *orlæg*, so too do families and clans, and these too affect the *orlæg* of the theod. As you can see, it can become very difficult to determine which deeds have impact and why. This is the very reason for law, traditions, and customs. By keeping to these things one can more readily ensure that nothing bad comes of the theod. Although wyrd can be altered by the runes, and by rites to the Gods and Goddesses, nothing is greater than deeds to keep it on a good course.

Chapter VII: Theod Structure

A theod is not a single entity. It is composed of many things. Theod structure varies from theod to theod, but generally a theod is consisted of shires, which in turn may be consisted of clans or families, and individuals. This is of course an oversimplification, but it is the best way to show the basic structure. Theods at the shire level are likely to have an assembly. There may be assemblies at lower levels. Some theods have moots which have their own assemblies. At theod level, there may be an Althing and a Witan. In some theods there may only be a Witan. The structure many theods used is outlined in Germania:

"Affairs of smaller moment the chiefs determine: about matters of higher consequence the whole nation deliberates; yet in such sort, that whatever depends upon the pleasure and decision of the people, is examined and discussed by the chiefs. Where no accident or emergency intervenes, they assemble upon stated days, either, when the moon changes, or is full: since they believe such seasons to be the most fortunate for beginning all transactions. Neither in reckoning of time do they count, like us, the number of days but that of nights. In this style their ordinances are framed, in this style their diets appointed; and with them the night seems to lead and govern the day. From their extensive liberty this evil and default flows, that they meet not at once, nor as men commanded and afraid to disobey; so that often the second day, nay often the third, is consumed through the slowness of the members in assembling. They sit down as they list, promiscuously, like a crowd, and all armed. It is by the Priests that silence is enjoined, and with the power of correction the Priests are then invested. Then the King or Chief is heard, as are others, each according to his precedence in age, or in nobility, or in warlike renown, or in eloquence; and the influence of every speaker proceeds rather from his ability to persuade than from any authority to command. If the proposition displease, they reject it by an inarticulate murmur: if it be pleasing, they brandish their javelins. The most honourable manner of signifying their assent, is to express their applause by the sound of their arms. (Tacitus Germania Chapter 11, Thomas Gordan translation)"

As can be seen the structure of the tribes described by Tacitus consisted of a chieftain, an assembly of chiefs, and an assembly of the freemen. This would correspond to the leader of a theod, its witan, and a folkmoot of the entire voting membership. Not all theods may do it this way. A valid alternative is to simply have a council or witan with no central leader. Still another alternative is for there to be no witan, but simply a folkmoot. All these variations are seen in the lore.

Miercinga Theod for example has at its head, an ealdorman, the ealdorman has an appointed witan. Then comes the folkmoot of the entire theod. Smaller units in the theod such as each *sætan* or shire have its own folkmoot, as do the mótas or moots of the *sætan*. Each assembly has its own powers. The ealdorman and the witan oversee the day to day operations of the entire theod. The folkmoot meets only on special occasions to discuss things of utmost importance to the theod, while the folkmoots of the *sætnas* meet only to determine their own course. The same is true of the mótas. The powers of each group vary according to their level. The folkmoot of a *mót* has not much power when it comes to the whole of Miercinga Theod. The folkmoot of the entire Miercinga Theod on the other hand can at times over rule the leadership of the theod. This is based in ancient Germanic precedent. According to the Saga of Olaf Haraldson, at a Thing held in Uppsala with King Olaf and his court present; Thorgny Lagman lectured King Olaf on the powers of the King and Thing. I quote it in part here:

"I also remember King Eirik the Victorious, and was with him on many a war-expedition. He enlarged the Swedish dominion, and defended it manfully; and it was also easy and agreeable to communicate our opinions to him. But the king we have now got allows no man to presume to talk with him, unless it be what he desires to hear. On this alone he applies all his power, while he allows his scat-lands in other countries to go from him through laziness and weakness. He wants to have the Norway kingdom laid under him, which no Swedish king before him ever desired, and therewith brings war and distress on many a man. Now it is our will, we bondes, that thou King Olaf make peace with the Norway king, Olaf the Thick, and marry thy daughter Ingegerd to him. Wilt thou, however, reconquer the kingdoms in the east countries which thy relations and forefathers had there, we will all for that purpose follow thee to the war. But if thou wilt not do as we desire, we will now attack thee, and put thee to death; for we will no longer suffer law and peace to be disturbed. So our forefathers went to work when they drowned five kings in a morass at the Mula-thing, and they were filled with the same insupportable pride thou hast shown towards us. Now tell us, in all haste, what resolution thou wilt take." Then the whole public approved, with clash of arms and shouts, the lagman's speech. The king stands up and says he will let things go according to the desire of the bondes. "All Swedish kings," he said, "have done so, and have allowed the bondes to rule in all according to their will."

(translator unknown, *Heimskringla*)

Here an Althing or folkmoot over rules the word of a king. So folkmoots are not without power. While generally a theod's leader and witan will propose things to the folkmoot to be done, or simply decide things in their own right, a folkmoot on rare occasion can state, "no, this is how it will be."

Chapter VIII: Hierarchy

"All men are created equal," how often do we here that phrase in the United States? The sad truth is that while all men may indeed be created equal, that equality quickly fades due to circumstances, social standing, and income. Within any society, it is almost nature for there to develop some form of hierarchy. Even in the United States, the home of the free, we speak of upper, middle, and lower classes. The sad truth is not all are equal.

Part of what Theodish Belief seeks to bring back is the social structure of the ancient Germanic tribes. This includes the social classes. At first, this may seem undesirable, until one stops and starts making comparisons to our modern situation. Position in ancient society could be earned or lost, just as it can be now. All that were free were guaranteed certain rights. And the higher the social position the more service a person had to provide for those below them. This is in a stark contrast to modern society where while we can earn or lose social position, while we are guaranteed certain rights, those of the upper class owe nothing to those of the lower classes. This makes ancient social structure somehow more desirable. One that has earned their position in a society and enjoy its privileges and pleasures should look out for those less fortunate. Theodish Belief believes those of higher social standing owe those of a lower social standing service of some kind. After all, those of a higher social standing would not be where they are had not someone of a lower standing put them there. Service may come in a variety of ways. It may mean gifts in symbel to those in one's hold or "under one's protection." It may mean teaching those new to the faith. It may mean ensuring financial security of those in one's hold. Service can take a variety of forms, but it must be there. If one in a high social position within a theod fails to do service, they are likely to soon lose that position.

Therefore positions within Theodism are earned through hard work, loyalty, and service. There are several ways at looking at it. One can see earning one's position in Theodish society as being like a Boy Scout earning badges. Or one can view it as a child taking more responsibility to earn more privileges. Position in Theodish society is earned. And with each step up the social ladder come more freedom, more privileges, and more service.

Freedom within Theodish society is earned in increments (and I am indebted to Êrmund Ethiling for this line of thought), much as it is in modern American society. One cannot see PG-13 movies until they are thirteen. One cannot drive until they are sixteen and have passed a driver's test. One cannot vote for another two years. And one cannot drink until they are twenty one. In most theods, there is a probationary membership level usually referred to as thralldom. The idea is that people entering into a theod have no rights, and therefore are no better than a thrall or slave. The terminology used differs according to theod. Some use cognates to Old English *þeow* slave, servant," while others use cognates to the Old English word *scealc*. It really does not matter what the lowest class is called. What matters are the concepts surrounding it are nearly the same in every theod. To quote Êrmund Ethiling on the topic:

"With the exception of those who are born into a thiod or who marry into Theodism, one's Theodish life begins in the institution of thiouudôm/theowdom. As a thio/theow, one sells his or herself into a period of servitude in which they start over and worth themselves anew. Thiouuos/theowes are by no means free in Theodish society. They are referred to as slaves, not permitted to have thiouuos of their own, are not given leave to make boasts in sumbal, have no vote or say at Thing, cannot participate in guilds or other institutions, are not permitted to bear arms, may not practice megin-craft, are given the larger portion of the grunt work at gatherings, and are, in many other ways, unfree. Thiouuos are considered to hold no worth or honor and why should they? Worth and honor are earned in Theodism after all, rather than just given out as a right afforded by one's existence.(Êrmund Ethiling, email to Saxon Theodish Belief Yahoo Group dated Feb. 24, 2007")

Thralls have no freedom in that they have no say in the running of the theod, no rights to do as they say. They do labor at religous gatherings. They do have a few guaranteed rights. They cannot be abused in any way. They can run away if they find Theodism is not for them. Beyond that they have no rights within the theod. Thralls earn their freedom over time, and this is referred to as worthing or "becoming." How they do this varies from theod to theod, but all require that the thrall must have learned the basics about Theodish Be-lief, and their place in it.

Above thralls is the first free class, which we will refer here to as churl. Again the terms used for it do not matter as much as the concept. In most theods, churls form the majority of the membership. A churl can vote in any folkmoot they may be a member of, can speak on nearly anything; can join a warband or guild. They cannot hold some offices, and cannot hold men of their own beyond their own family. They cannot lead a warband or guild. In some theods there are several levels of churl, the higher ones being able to hold certain offices, and have men in hold to him or her (thus being able to lead a guild or warband).

The next class is generally referred to as thane, and nearly all theods use a cognate of Old English *þegn* although some use Old English *gesíþa*. For some theods it is the highest social level or *árung* or "honoring," while others hold it to be the second highest. Thane is the first level where service is truly required. Thanes generally hold some sort of office, and are in service to their folk and to the lord they are hold to. In ancient Heathenry, thanes had folk they had to oversee and protect, and owed the king some form of military service, as well as maintenance of bridges and fortresses. Within modern Theodish Belief they perform much of the duties that keep the theod running. They organize gatherings, run websites, and operate mailing lists.

Above thane is what we will call lord. Some theods use the office of ealdorman to fulfill this *árung*, others have it as an *árung* separate from the office, while some theods do not have the office at all. Again what they call it may vary. Some may use the term ealdorman, others *hláford*. A lord is a leader of a folk of good number. They will have several thanes oathed to them, and their thanes will have men of their own. A lord is likely to have a seat on the witan of a theod, and therefore take care of some large part of theod business. With their privileges they will also have many responsibilities as they are in greater debt to the people that put them where they are. Above lord is the king. As of now, only two theods have ever had kings. The first was the Winland Ríce who raised Garman Lord to that level. The second was Sahsisk Thíod that temporarily made Êrmund Ethiling king during a conflict with another theod (as it is Old Saxon custom to only have kings in time of war). Most therefore use an ealdorman in placed of a king as a sort of "chairman of the witan." Kingship will be covered in more detail in Chapter IX.

One can move freely up or down the social level. A lord that has failed his or her folk may find that they have become a thane. A churl that has done exceptionally well in service to the theod may find the folk clamoring they be made a thane. All have the same basic rights, not unlike our own Bill of Rights we live under in the United States.

Chapter IX: The Web of Oaths

Within modern Theodism it has always been accepted that a theod needs something to bond it together. Within ancient tribes it was common descent from some ancient ancestor and bonds of kinship that generally forged the bonds that held the tribe together. Modern theods are not so fortunate, so another way had to be sought to tie the theod together. Thus was born the concept of the web of oaths. In ancient times, unrelated persons could be united in an artificial brotherhood in the form of a *dryht* or warband, or a gild or guild. Within the warband or guild, the lord or *dryhten* of the warband or guild was seen as a fatherhood figure with the warband or guild as a sort of band of brothers. The veterans of the warband or guild held more say than the youths as would be the case in a family with the eldest family members having more say than the youngest . For the warband or guild to operate as an artificial family however there had to be some form of bonding. The core of a *dryht* or gild would often be true kinsmen, and for them no artificial bonds were needed. But for others, there had to be a substitute for the bonds of kinship created by birth into an extended family. This substitute was the hold oath. Hold oaths bond people together in must the way kinship does, and therefore are seen as having the same strengths of kinship.

Hold oaths hold certain obligations. The thane agrees to in some way serve the lord. This is likely to be in a specific form of service. For example in modern Theodism one might agree to run a website. Or it may be just a very general agreement of any kind of service.

In return, the lord will be free with gifts to the thane. These gifts can often be very simple or of great value. The exchange of gifts and service further strengthens the bond of the hold oath. Over time as service and gifts are exchanged the bonds may become as strong as that of kinship. The web of oaths bonds the theod together in that one thane is oathed to a lord, who in turn is oathed to another lord, ultimately ending with the ealdorman, *dryhten*, or *cyning* of the theod. Hold oaths are not the only way a theod is bond together. There are of course marriages, relation by blood, and blood brotherhood, but hold oaths are by far the most common way.

Chapter X: Sacral Leadership

Sacral leadership is something every theod believes in, yet finds hard to define. The sacral leader is seen as holding or warding the luck of the tribe, and to have certain duties such as bloting. But beyond these sacral leadership is largely a shadowy area of Theodism, little understood, and hard to explain. Therefore, this chapter is going to try to approach it from the framework of history. For ease, the aspects of sacral kingship will be outlined.

1) The sacral king was responsible for the luck of the tribe. He generated it, protected it, and could loan it if need be. According to the scholar William Chaney:

"The king is above all the intermediary between his people and the gods. The charismatic embodiment of the 'luck' of the folk.(William Chaney" *The Cult of Kingship* Berkeley: University of California Press, pages11-12)"

In the *Heimskringla* and the sagas, kings often lend their *hamingja* or luck to others.

2) The sacral king had to partake in the sacred feasts. This is seen in the *Heimskringla*, where Hakon the Good, a Christian king tolerant of Heathens, had to take part in Heathen feasts to keep his folk happy.

"The relation of the divine and the tribal is primarily one of action, of 'doing,' and to assure the favourable

75

actions of the gods toward the tribe the kinf 'does' his office as mediator between them, sacrificing for victory, for good crops, and for peace….(William Chaney" *The Cult of Kingship* Berkeley: University of California Press, page 12)"

Heathen kings had to perform blot to ensure the good luck of the tribe continued.

3) The sacral king can trace their ancestry back ultimately to a deity. With most of the Anglo-Saxon kings this was Woden, but the kings of Essex traced themselves to Seaxneat. The Swedeish kings traced themselves to Frea (Frey).

4) The sacral king represented the tribe, the tribal identity was one with the king's. Herwig Wulfram has this to say:

"The early Germanic thiudans personified the tribe in a very real way. His tribe saw him the best man to please the gods of war and nature because of his Heil, that certain nsomething about him the ancient deities liked. His tribe entrusted him with thei very identity: the divine liking for him meant a greater probability of victory or survival in face of calamity than tribesmen could hope for on their merits" (Henry Meyers and Herwig Wolfram, *Medieval Kingship*, Burnham Inc Publishing, page 348)

The sacral king is the tribe as a whole's representative to the Gods and Goddesses. This is especially true when the king sacrificed to the deities. In return via the king, the Gods and Goddesses would reward tribe, for example with victory in battle. It was also true when the king sought the guidance of the Ése (Æsir) and Wen (Vanir).

5) The sacral king had the gift of *ræd*, or advice from the Gods. This can be seen in the *Flateyjarbók* where King Eric consults the idol of a deity called Lýtir. The idol is lead through a procession in a wagon. The wagon ends at the king's hall, where the king sacrifices and then, questions the idol. Kings also took other auguries:

"But to this nation it is peculiar, to learn presages and admonitions divine from horses also. These are nourished by the State in the same sacred woods and groves, all milk-white and employed in no earthly labour. These yoked in the holy chariot, are accompanied by the Priest and the King, or the Chief of the Community, who both carefully observed his actions and neighing. (Gordon translation, Tacitus, *Germania*)

They interpreted omens and sat on the mounds of their ancestors to receive inspiration. As H.R. Ellis says in *Road to Hel:*

"Is it accidental that the apple sent by Frigg, the eating of which by his queen brings them a child, drops in the king's lap while he sits on a howe? And again it is while sitting on a howe that the young Helgi, for whom no name be found, receives one at last. (H.R. Ellis, *The Road to Hel,* New York: Green Wood Press, page 107)"

What this means for Theodism is that the leader of a theod is seen as a sacral leader. They hold the luck of the tribe, and serve as the folk's representative to the Ése (Æsir) and Wen (Vanir). As such, the sacral leader must fain the deities to gain their favor. They commune with the Gods and ancestors. Sacral leadership is central to Theodish Belief. The leadership is elected by the folk and it is their place to guide the folk. They do this in the same way the kings of old did. They take omens, read the runes, watch for signs that what they are doing is right. They fain and blot regularly, and interact with both the Gods and the folk. In addition, they are armed with all the skills to be a modern leader. It is not uncommon for a Theodish leader to take training in counseling or mediation in order to be able to help their folk through a crisis, or mediate disputes within the tribe and thus maintain the frith. They learn to organize gatherings, and to conduct public relations for the tribe. Finally, they learn to be good managers, appointing the right people for the right jobs, and making sure everything runs smoothly. Being a leader of a theod is not an easy task, and it takes a very special person to do it. Both women and wermen are chosen as leaders. Women are especially liked for their intuition and their sacred innate ability to commune with the Gods and ancestors.

Sacral leadership, especially in this day and age is no easy task. With so much of the lore forever lost, the leadership of today is cut off from many of the rites the sacral king must have performed to maintain their office. A leader in a modern theod must be able to attract new folk to the theod, ensure that the theod's members prosper, perform blot, in addition to exhibit the traditional leadership skills required. If they fail in this, they can be removed from office, and a new leader chosen to take their place. A sacral leader is not seen as a king, but they are seen as one step below one. Someday, most Theodish groups may have kings, but for now only one theod does

Chapter XI: Innangards

The ancient Heathens viewed the world as that within their sphere of influence and that without. According to Kirsten Hastrup:

"The important point is that in our period a structural and semantic opposition was operative between "inside" and "outside" the society-as-law, allowing for a merging of different kinds of beings in the conceptual "wild." This anti-social space was inhabited by a whole range of spirits...landsvættir "spirits of the land," huldufolk "hidden people," jötnar "giants," trölls "trolls," and álfar "elves"...all of them belonged to the "wild" and it was partly against them that one had to defend oneself... In this way the secure, well-known and personal innangards was symbolically separated from the dangerous unknown and nonhuman wild space outside the fence, útangards. (Kirsten Hastrup, *Culture and History in Medieval Iceland: An Anthropological Analysis of Structure and Change*, Oxford: Claredon Press)

The *innangards* (ON) is all that is within the nine worlds. Outside is the *útangards* (ON), the wilds where man has no control. Thus you have the nine worlds, and then Útgard; that outside the sphere of both Man and the Gods (as well as the giants, elves, and dwarves). It is a place where creatures such as Útgard Loki dwell. The ancient Heathens applied this reasoning to their social units as well as Mankind as a whole. They viewed the world of man as a farmstead with its enclosing fences. All inside the world of Man was inside the fences. This applied to tribes, who were viewed as their own enclosures. The law of Mercia did not apply to someone from Northumbria even if the crime was committed in Mercia. Each tribe was its own *innangards* (ON). Each had its own law code. Each had its own customs and traditions. Each had its own assembly and leadership. The tribe was seen much as a farmstead, separate from all that was around it. Bauschatz touches on an idea similar to *innangards* (ON) in relation to Wyrd and deeds:

"For the Germanic peoples, space as it is encountered and perceived in the created worlds of men and other beings, exists, to any significant degree only as a location or container for the occurrence of action...The container is action, whether of individual men, of men acting in consort or in opposition, of men and monsters, or whatever. In all cases, immediate actions are discontinuous and separable deriving power and structure from the past. (Paul Bauschatz, *The Well and the Tree: World and Time in Early Germanic Culture*, Amherst: The University of Massachusetts Press)"

The enclosure of the *innangards* (ON) includes not only the wermen and women that inhabit it, but also their actions. It is a container for *orlæg* and *mægen* as well. All that is related to the tribe is a part of the *innangards* (ON) whether it be deed, thought, or belief.

  For Theodish Belief, the *innangards* (ON) is the theod, the tribe that one is a member of. The deeds done within the theod are the deeds of the theod. Its members are separated from the outside world by the virtue of their being theodsmen. Just as there are spiritual correspondences between the individual and the family, so too are there between the tribe and the family, and the tribe and the individual.

The ancient Heathens viewed that outside the tribe as suspect, not necessarily to be trusted. Thus Old English *wearg* meant not only "outlaw" but "evil" as well. Similarly, Old Norse *fiandR* "outsider" was cognate to Old English *féond* "demon," our word "fiend." Outlaws, those literally outside the protection of the law, could be killed without fear of intercession by the assembly or any type of retribution. While modern Theodsmen do not take this view, they do rely more on the word of their fellow tribe members.

This outside vs. inside is central to Theodish Belief. The theod is designed to be a self contained unit. Its leadership and members control all that goes on within it, decides whose its members are, decides its customs, its thews, its structure. Outsiders have little impact on what goes on in a theod. The theod is under its own sphere of influence, and no one else's. In a way this is no different than any organization, save in Theodish Belief, the theod's separateness is stressed.

The theod consists of smaller enclosures such as "shires," clans, and families. Each has their own particular customs, thews, and traditions. Each has its own *orlæg* in addition to that of the tribe. Within these smaller enclosures, their leadership reigns supreme. The tribe does not interfere with what goes on in the halls of one of its shires. Within a family's home the head of household takes the high seat in symbel regardless of what tribal dignitaries are present. The tribe does not interfere with household affairs. Each entity of the theod has a right to govern its self within its own realm

82

of being. This varies from theod to theod, but for the most part it is true. Often you will hear something referred to as a "rooftree matter," which means it is a matter of concern to a family, and not to be meddled with by anyone outside the family.

The concept of *innangards* (ON) impacts much of how a theod operates. The whole reason for people coming in as a thrall or a *þéow* is because they must integrate with the tribe. They have no past deeds with the theod to draw upon, and are coming in as an outsider. In order to integrate with the theod, they must perform deeds that will lead to their being accepted as a part of it. That is, they must become a part of the theod's *orlæg*. Were they to enter as a freeman, then, they would have the potential of seriously damaging the theod as they are still essentially an outsider with no deeds done within the theod to draw upon. Therefore, thralldom is a way of gradually easing into the theod by doing deeds within the enclosure of the theod. As mentioned before "rooftree issues" are another outgrowth of the concept of *innangards* (ON), as is the idea that the tribe is an entity unto its self.

Chapter XII: Worship

There are two major forms of worship in Theodism. One is commonly called faining, and consists of a libation of mead or the giving of another gift such as a sword. The other is blót, the gifting of an animal to the Gods and Goddesses. They use the same basic outline, the only difference being in the gift. Different theods use different outlines, but the basic premises are the same. We give to the Gods and Goddesses to get something in return.

The reasons for faining or blót are basically the same. We give to the Gods and Goddesses for gifts in return. The ancient Heathens gifted the Gods and Goddesses for the same reason. In *Fjölsviðmál*, it is said:

Tell me, Fjolsvith For I wish to know;
answer as I do ask
do they help award to their worshippers,
if need of help they have?

Ay they help award to their worshippers,
in hallowed stead if they stand;
there is never a need That neareth a man
but they lend a helping hand.
(Fjölsviðmál, Hollander translation 39 and 40)

In *Hynduljóð* the idea of men being rewarded for blot is touched upon as well:

He a high altar made me Of heaped stones–
all glary have grown The gathered rocks–

and reddened anew them with neats' fresh blood;
for ay believed Óttar in the ásynjur.
(Hynduljóð, Hollander translation verse 10)

Similar statements appear in the sagas as well. In *Víga-Glúms Saga*, Þorkell states Frey had "accepted many gifts from him" and "repaid them well."

Faining therefore plays an important role in Theodism. By giving to the Gods and Goddesses, the theod as a whole seeks to increase the tribal luck. Faining can also be done in return for gifts already given, as a form of thanks. Fainings are generally done on the holytides, which vary from theod to theod (and for that reason will not be named here). Blót is generally only done on a high holytide such as Yule.

Blót is the highest of Theodish rites, and a bit of the reasoning behind it needs to be explained. The greatest gift one can give to the Gods and Goddesses is a life. The animal must be one carefully nurtured, and therefore prepared for the rite. It is treated with respect and care. The act of blót itself or the slaying is humane. The jugular vein is cut, and the animal dies painlessly in seconds. In this respect it is done in the same way as the Jews do for kosher meat. It is far more humane than modern slaughterhouses use (which is why the slaying is handled by the theod and not a professional). Once the animal is slain and the blood caught for the blessing, the animal is butchered for the ritual feast or húsel. The húsel is a sharing of meat and drink with the Gods and Goddess. The most favorable parts of the animal is reserved for the Ése (Æsir) and Wen (Vanir). Blót and húsel are much more like a sacralized pig roast than anything else.

Sharing food and drink with the Gods and Goddesses are a form of bonding. The exchange of food and drink is an act of friendship, and a way of creating links to the Gods and Goddesses stronger than your average libation. It is a way of building relationships with the deities.

Not great things alone must one give to another,
praise oft is earned for nought;
with half a loaf and a tilted bowl
I have found me many a friend.
(Havamal 53, Bray translation)

Hast thou a friend whom thou trustest well,
from whom thou cravest good?
Share thy mind with him, gifts exchange with him,
fare to find him oft.
(Havamal 44 Bray translation)

Vilhelm Grönbech furthers this idea of gifting as a form of bonding:

"When an article of value is passed across the boundary of frith and grasped by alien hands, a fusion of life takes place, which binds men one to another with an obligation of the same character as that of frith its self." (Grönbech. *The Culture of the Teutons*, Vol.2, p. 55)"

As said earlier, the greatest gift one can give the Gods and Goddesses is that of a life. In this blot is a form of communion, sharing with the Gods and Goddesses.

"The meaning of the sacrificial feast, as Snorri saw it, is fairly plain. When blood was sprinkled over altars and men and the toasts were drunk, men were symbolically joined with gods of war and fertility, and with their dead ancestors, sharing their mystical powers. This is a form of communion." (Turville-Petre. *Myth and Religion of the North*, p. 251).

For an instant in time, men and deities are in the same space, partaking of the same food, sharing, to a small degree, the same power. This is the reason why animal sacrifice is practiced in Theodism. Food other than a slain animal could be used, such as meat bought from a supermarket, but if the animal it came from had been mistreated, the deities may take offense. Therefore Theodsmen prefer to slay their own.

The outline of faining or worship consists of some basic actions taken from the *Hákonar Saga* in the *Heimskringla*, the only detailed source of information on the rite.

Það var forn siður þá er blót skyldi vera að allir bændur skyldu þar koma sem hof var og flytja þannug föng sín, þau er þeir skyldu hafa meðan veislan stóð. Að veislu þeirri skyldu allir menn öl eiga. Þar var og drepinn alls konar smali og svo hross en blóð það allt er þar kom af, þá var kallað hlaut og hlautbollar það er blóð það stóð í, og hlautteinar, það var svo gert sem stökklar, með því skyldi rjóða stallana öllu saman og svo veggi hofsins utan og innan og svo stökkva á mennina en slátur skyldi sjóða til mannfagnaðar. Eldar skyldu vera á miðju gólfi í hofinu og þar katlar yfir. Skyldi full um eld bera en sá er gerði veisluna og

höfðingi var, þá skyldi hann signa fullið og allan blót-
matinn. Skyldi fyrst Óðins full, skyldi það drekka til
sigurs og ríkis konungi sínum, en síðan Njarðar full og
Freys full til árs og friðar. Þá var mörgum mönnum títt
að drekka þar næst bragafull. Menn drukku og full
frænda sinna, þeirra er heygðir höfðu verið, og voru það
minni kölluð.

"It was an old custom, that when there was to be sacrifice all the bondes should come to the spot where the
temple stood and bring with them all that they required
while the festival of the sacrifice lasted. To this festival
all the men brought ale with them; and all kinds of cattle, as well as horses, were slaughtered, and all the
blood that came from them was called "hlaut", and the
vessels in which it was collected were called hlaut-
vessels. Hlaut-staves were made, like sprinkling
brushes, with which the whole of the altars and the
temple walls, both outside and inside, were sprinkled
over, and also the people were sprinkled with the blood;
but the flesh was boiled into savoury meat for those
present. The fire was in the middle of the floor of the
temple, and over it hung the kettles, and the full goblets
were handed across the fire; and he who made the feast,
and was a chief, blessed the full goblets, and all the
meat of the sacrifice. And first Odin's goblet was emptied for victory and power to his king; thereafter,
Niord's and Frey's goblets for peace and a good season.
Then it was the custom of many to empty the brage-
goblet; and then the guests emptied a goblet to the
memory of departed friends, called the remembrance
goblet." (*Hákonar Saga goða, Heimskringla*)

The rite described can be roughly outlined as below. Keep in mind, that this outline may vary from theod to theod.

1) Preparations: Any preparations for the faining are made. This may mean setting up the area for faining, or gathering the folk.

2) Creation of sacred space: Sacred space is created through a variety of means available to the theods.

3) Blót: If an animal is being offered it is then slain.

4) Blessing: The folk, and altar are sprinkled with a blot-tine.

5) Hallowing of the mead and/or meat: The food and/or drink to be gifted is passed over fire to hallow it. Note, that not all theods do this.

6) The Bedes or Fulls: Toasts are drunk to the Gods and Goddesses being gifted. These are done in the form of prayers.

7) *Myne*: The ancestors are drank to.

8) Húsel: The sacred feast its self. In the case of a libation this is when the mead would be drank, and toasts would be made.

9) Yielding or Gifting: The food and/or drink is given to the Gods and Goddesses.

As stated before this outline will vary from theod to theod. Some elements may not appear at all, while other elements may be added. The order may be different. But the basic premise behind all Theodish fainings are the same.

Chapter XIII: Symbel

Symbel is the other major rite of Theodish Belief. It is well preserved appearing in *Béowulf*, the *Heimskringla*, the *Fagrskinna, , Lokasenna*, and mentioned in passing in many of the Icelandic sagas. The speech in symbel revolves around deeds. Past deeds, deeds one intends to do, and deeds of one's ancestors all play a role. The scholar Paul Bauscatz states there are three activities that take place at symbel:

"With respect to the symbel, only three types of activity are central: drinking (and in related actions such as passing the cup), speech (with the related recitation and singing), and gift giving." (Paul Bauschatz, *The Well and the Tree: World and Time in Early Germanic Culture*, Amherst: The University of Massachusetts Press, page 74)

The purpose of symbel is to place one's self in contact with Wyrd. Indeed, Bauschatz sees the rite as symbolic of the actions of the *Wyrdæ*:

"This combination of words, their denoted actions, and the semantic elements of the drink and cup repeat the whole act of the continual speaking of the *ørlög* and the nurturing of the tree Yggdrasil, the central activities of the Norns" (." (Paul Bauschatz, The Well and the Tree: World and Time in Early Germanic Culture, Amherst: The University of Massachusetts Press, page 78)

The horn is symbolic of the Well of Wyrd; the drinking the watering of the tree, and the speech, the speaking of *orlæg*. Thus to a degree, those taking part in symbel are trying to alter wyrd, or to control it in some way. They boast of past actions that have successful conclusions in hopes that deeds they vow to do will turn out the same.

Symbel like faining consists of certain ritual actions. Primary amongst these are the *gielp* and *béot* . In the first *Béowulf* symbel for example, Béowulf tells who his father is and states that in his youth he has undertaken many great deeds. This is a *gielp*. Béowulf then makes his boast to slay the creature terrorizing Héorot. This is his *béot* . A *gielp* is a boast of one's ancestry and past deeds. The *béot* is a vow to do something. These are sacred oaths, not to be entered into lightly.

There are other ritual actions such as the *minni* (ON) or *myne*, a toast to one's ancestors. Formally, these consist of a round near the beginning of symbel, but they can be made at anytime during the symbel. The final form of ritual speech is that of the *léoþ*. The *léoþ* is a song or tale of significance. It can be a tale of the ancestors, or a song dedicated to the Gods and Goddesses. Another ritual action is that of *flítung* or *senna* (ON). A *flítung* is basically an insult contest between two members of the symbel. It is rare, and can be ended by the *symbelgifa*, the *þyle* (more on these positions below), or by the participants. It can follow several patterns, the most common of which is insult for insult. But in Béowulf, Béowulf responds to Unferþ with a boast, and then an insult. *Flítung* is a serious matter, and is not to be undertaken unless one means the words they intend to say. One must also be ready to back up their words in any number of ways. The prime examples of *Flítung* are Loki's words in the *Lokasenna*, and the exchange between Béowulf and Unferþ in *Béowulf*. Finally, the idea that the horn must first pass through the hands of a woman as they are sacred, is another ritual action.

Symbel seating is in a precise order. The lord and lady of the hall are seated at the high seat. Those of highest *árung* are seated closest to them in the order of their *árung* going from highest being closest, and lowest being farthest away. If there is a particularly honored guest, they may be seated at a guest high seat directly opposite that of the lord and lady.

There are also certain offices associated with symbel. The *symbelgifa* is the host of the hall, the one who makes the initial fulls, and decides when symbel is concluded. The *symbelgifa* may lend their speed to any vow made in hall. The *ealubora* is the highest ranking lady who serves the initial rounds. Women are considered sacred, and to have the gift of foresight that wermen do not. Because of this they can advise those about to boast as to an idea of what they are in for. The *þyle* sees to it that all boasts are done in a serious manner and challenges any vow they may feel will go unfulfilled. Where the *ealubora* flatters, the *þyle* insults. Finally, a *byrele* is any young werman or woman that serves the mead after the initial rounds. There can be other offices such as *duruþegn* or door thane, a guard at the door to make sure the rite is not disturbed; *gléoman* or singer, and the *scop*, or poet.

Symbel can follow one of two patterns. One is referred to as High Symbel, and it is the form presented here. Symbel generally follows the following outline. Again, with so much of this book, it must be stated that it may vary from theod to theod. The outline for these opening rounds are drawn from Steven Pollington's work, *The Mead-Hall* pages 42 to 47 with additional elements added from Eric Wodening's outline seen in *An Anglo-Saxon Symbel.*

1) Summoning - The guests are summoned to the hall by a horn. Pollington notes that on the Bayeux Tapestry, a horn blower is shown.

2) Entrance of Guests into the Hall - The guests enter and wash their hands. Pollington points to a verse from the *Havamal,* "Water and handcloth and friendly word, a chance to speak, guest friendship will he gladly find, kindness and attention" (Pollington, p. 42).

3) Seating - The *symbelgifa* as in regular symbel seats each person according to arung. The *symbelgifa* then takes the position before the high seat.

4) Symbelgifa Forespeach - The *symbelgifa* opens symbel with words similar to those from Béowulf lines 489-490: "Sitaþ nu to symle ond onsælaþ meoto, sige-hreð secgum, swa þin sefas hwettaþ (Sit now to symbel and unwind your measures, victory hearted heroes)," and then sits down. If folks are not already seated they should do so at this point.

5) *Ealubora* Forespeach - The *ealubora* then enters with the horn and mead. She greets all present, and then presents the *symbelgifa* with the horn. According to

Pollington, Enright, and others this may have involved a ritual formula much like Wealtheow's words in Béowulf lines 1169-1175: "Onfoh þissum fulle, freodrihten min, sinces brytta! þu on sælum wes, gold-wine gumena, ond to Geatum spræc mildum wordum... (Take this full, my lord *dryhten*, hoard sharer, you be happy, warriors' gold friend, and speak to the Geats with mild words...)"

6) Bregofull - The *symbelgifa* then performs the boasts to the three gods and goddesses worshipped by his or her household, followed by a *minni* to the ancestors, and finally, the bregofull, a boast of what his or her folk will do in the coming year.

7) Guest Speech - If there is a guest of arung close to the *symbelgifa*, they are then given the right of guest speech. The *ealubora* will take the horn to them, and they will greet the *symbelgifa*, and make a *béot* (which may be a boast to help the *symbelgifa* or his or her own folk in some way, a *minni* in praise of the gods, or simply a toast of some sort). The *þyle* may of course challenge (as they may anyone save the *ealubora* and *symbelgifa*).

8) The First Full - The *ealubora* then takes the horn to each person by arung. They may make a *béot*, boast to the Gods, or ancestors. The *ealubora* then takes their seat, and the task of carrying the horn about is taken over by the *byreles*.

9) Gift giving (optional) - The *symbelgifa* may then give gifts to those present. Theoretically this can be done at anytime during symbel however

10) Léoð (optional) - The *scop* may then sing a song, either in praise of the gods, the folk, or the *symbelgifa*.

11) The Fulls - From here on High Symbel has open rounds in which nearly anything can be done. People may make a *gielp* and *béot*, sing a song, toast someone, recite poetry, even tell jokes. The *þyle*, of course, can challenge any boast. The *ealubora* may also decide to pour mead for anyone at any time along with flattering speech.

The simpler form of symbel dispenses with these initial rounds, and begins instead with a round to the Gods where the horn is passed to each and every person who then boasts the deity of their choice, the ancestors where the same is done, and finally a round for friends and family with open fulls following.

Index

Bibliography

Aswynn, Freya. Leaves of Yggdrasil. (St. Paul, MN: Llewellyn)

Bauschatz, Paul. The Well and the Tree (Amherst, MA: University of Massachusetts Press, 1982)

Blain, Jenny Nine Worlds of Seid-Magic: Ecstasy and Neo-Shamanism in North European Paganism, (Routledge, 2001)

Bosworth, Joseph; T.Northcote Toller. An Anglo-Saxon Dictionary and An Anglo-Saxon Dictionary: Supplement. (Oxford, England: Oxford University Press).

Branston, Brian. Gods of the North (London: Thames & Hudson, 1955)

Branston, Brain. Lost Gods of England (London: Thames and Hudson)

Byock, Jesse (tr.). Saga of the Volsungs. (Berkeley, CA : University of California Press)

Cæsar, Julius; S.A. Handford, tr. The Conquest of Gaul (Penguin Books, 1982).

Chaney, William. The Cult of Kingship in Anglo-Saxon England (Berkeley, CA: University of California Press, 1970)

Chisholm, James, Grove and Gallows (Austin TX: Rune-Gild, 1987).

Cleasby, Richard; Gudbrand Vigfusson, An Icelandic-English Dictionary (Oxford, England: Oxford University Press)

Conquergood, Dwight. "Boasting in Anglo-Saxon England, Performance, and the Heroic Ethos". Literature and Performance, vol. I, April 1991, pp. 24-35.

DaSant, George W.(tr.) Njal's Saga ((London, 1861)

Elliot, R.W.V. Runes, (Manchester, England: Manchester University Press)

Ellis-Davidson, H.R. Gods and Myths of Northern Europe. (New York, NY: Viking-Penguin)

Ellis-Davidson, H.R. Myths and Symbols in Pagan Europe. (New York: University of Syracuse Press: Syracuse).

Ellis, H.R. The Road to Hel (Cambridge: Cambridge University Press, 1943; rep. Greenwood Press, 1977).

Gloseki, Stephen. Shamanism and Old English Poetry (New York: Garland Publishing, 1989).

Grammaticus, Saxo; Oliver Elton (tr.) The Danish History (Norroena Society, 1905).

Grattan, John Henry Grafton. and Charles Singer. Anglo-Saxon Magic and Medicine (Norwood, PA: Norwood Editions, 1976).

Griffiths, Bill, Aspects of Anglo-Saxon Magic (Norfolk: Anglo-Saxon Books, 1999)

Grimm, Jacob; James Stallybrass (tr.) Teutonic Mythology (4 vols.).
(Magnolia, MA: Peter Smith Publishing)

Grönbech, Vilhelm. Culture of the Teutons (London: Oxford University Press, 1931).

Gundarsson., Kveldulf Teutonic Religion (St. Paul, MN: Llewellyn,1996)

Hastrup, Kirsten. Culture and History in Mediæval Iceland (Oxford: Clarendon Press, 1985)

Hallakarva , Gunnora "Courtship, Love and Marriage in Viking Scandinavia"
(http://vikinganswerlady.org [Electronic version])

Hastrup, Kirsten, Culture and History in Medieval Iceland: An Anthropological Analysis of Structure and Change, (Oxford: Press 1985)

Hodge, Winifred, "On the Meaning of Frith" (Lina, Midsummer 1996)

Hollander, Lee. The Poetic Edda. (Austin, TX: University of Texas Press)

Lang, Samuel (tr.) *Heimskringla*: A History of the Norse Kings (London: Norroena Society, 1907)

Owen, Gale R. Rites and Religions of the Anglo-Saxons (Dorset Press, 1985)

Page, R.I. An Introduction to English Runes, (London: Methuen and Co.)

Paxson, Diana, "The Matronæ" (Sage Woman, Fall, 1999)

Paxson, Diana "The Return of the Völva: Recovering the Practice of Seidh
(Mountain Thunder, Summer, 1993)

Polomé, Edgar C. Essays on Germanic Religion (Washington: Institute for
the Study of Man, 1989).

Press, Muriel (tr.) Laxdaela Saga (London: The Temple Classics, 1899)

Schwartz, Stephen P. Poetry and Law in Germanic Myth (Berkeley: University of California Press, 1973)

Storms, Anglo-Saxon Magic (The Hague: Martinus Nijhoff, 1948)

Sturluson, Snorri ; Anthony Faulkes (tr.). Edda. (Rutland VT : Everyman's
Press)

Snorri Sturluson; Erling Monsen, A.H. Smith (trs., eds). *Heimskringla*.
(New York, NY: Dover Publications: Inc).

101

Storms, Dr. G. Anglo-Saxon Magic (The Hague: Martinus Nijhoff, 1948).

Tacitus, Cornelius. Agricola, Germania, Dialogus. Loeb Classics Library
ed., (Cambridge, MA: Harvard University Press)

Thorsson, Edred, A Book of Troth (St. Paul, MN: Llewellyn)

Turville-Petre, E.O.G. Myth and Religion of the North. (Westport, CT: Greenwood Publishing Group)

Wallace-Hadrill, J.M., Early Germanic Kingship in England and on the Continent (Oxford: University of Oxford Press)

Wilson, David. Anglo-Saxon Paganism (New York, NY: Routledge, 1992)

Wilson, David M. (ed.) The Archaeology of Anglo-Saxon England (Cambridge: University Press, 1981)

Wodening, Eric, "The Meaning of Frith" (Ásatrú Today, December 1994)

Wodening, Eric, We Are Our Deeds: The Elder Heathenry, its Ethic and Thew (Watertown, NY: THEOD, 1998)

Wodening, Swain, Beyond Good and Evil: Germanic Heathen Ethics (Watertown, NY: THEOD, 1994)

Wodening, Swain, Hammer of the Gods: Anglo-Saxon Paganism in Modern Times (Little Elm, TX: Miercinga Theod, 2004)

Wolfram, Herwig, Medieval Kingship, (Burnham Inc Publishing)

Appendix

An Alternative Worship Outline

Most are familiar with blót which although covered by dozens of Heathen writers always looks almost the same. What most do not realize is there is an alternative to that outline, one which is more flexible in its usages. The Æcer Bót (also known as the "Field Remedy" or "For Unfruitul Land") is found in an Anglo-Saxon work known as the Lácunga or "Leech Cunning." It is a semi-Christianized rite that is thought pagan in origin. It is also the only rite to survive in the Anglo-Saxon corpus, and perhaps the only one to survive outside of the sacrifices detailed in the *Heimskringla*. Never the less, it has rarely been looked to as an alternative to the standard blót outline (which although used for libations does not adapt well to that usage). It is given below:

Metrical Charm 1: For Unfruitful Land

Here is the solution, how you may improve your fields if the are not fertile, or if anything unwholesome has been done to them through sorcery or witchcraft.

At night, before dawn, take four turfs from the four quarters of your lands, and note how they previously stood. Then take oil and honey and yeast and milk from every cow that is in the land, and part of every kind of tree grown on the land, except hard beams, and part of every identifiable herb except the buckbean only, and add to them holy water.

Then drip it three times on the base of the turfs, and say these words: Crescite, grow, et multiplicamini, and multiply, et replete, and fill, terre, this earth. In nomine patris et filii et spiritus sancti sit benedicti. And say the Lord's Prayer as often as the other.

And then take the turfs to church and let a priest sing four masses over them, and let the green surface be turned towards the altar, and then, before sunset, let the turfs be brought to the places where they were previously. And let the man have four crosses of quickbeam made for him, and write upon each end: Matthew and Mark, Luke and John. Lay the crucifix on the bottom of the pit, then say: Crux Matheus, crux Marcus, crux Lucas, crux sanctus Iohannes. Then take the turfs and set them down there, and say these words nine times, 'Crescite' as before, and the Lord's Prayer as often, and then turn eastward, and humbly bow down nine times, and then say these words:

Eastward I stand, entreating favours,
I pray the glorious Lord, I pray the great Lord,
I pray the holy warden of heaven,
Earth I pray and heaven above
And the steadfast, saintly Mary
And heaven's might and highest hall
That by grace of God I might this glamour
Disclose with teeth. Through trueness of thought
Awaken these plants for our worldly profit,
Fill these fields through firm belief,
Make these fields pleasing, as the prophet said

That honour on earth has he who dutifully
deals out alms, doing God's will.

Then turn yourself three times awiddershins, then
stretch out flat and there intone the litanies. Then say;
Sanctus, sanctus, sanctus to the end: then sing the
Benedicte with arms extended, and the Magnificat, and
the Lord's Prayer three times, and commend it to Christ
and Saint Mary and the Holy Cross, for love and for
reverence, and for the grace of him who owns the land,
and all those who are under him. When all that is done,
then take unfamiliar seeds from beggars and give them
twice as much as you took from them, and let him
gather all his plough apparatus together; then let him
bore a hole in the plough beam and put in there styrax
and fennel and hallowed soap and hallowed salt. Then
take the seed, set it on the plough's body, then say:

Erce, Erce, Erce, Mother of Earth,
May the Almighty grant you, the Eternal Lord,
Fields sprouting and springing up,
Fertile and fruitful,
Bright shafts of shining millet,
And broad crops of barley
And white wheaten crops
And all the crops of earth.
May God Almighty grant the owner,
(And his hallows who are in heaven),
That his land be fortified against all foes,
And embattled against all evil,
From sorceries sown throughout the land.
Now I pray the Wielder who made this world
That no cunning woman, nor crafty man,

May weaken the words that are uttered here.

Then drive forward the plough and cut the first furrow, then say:

Hail, Earth, mother of all;
Be abundant in God's embrace,
Filled with food for our folk's need.

Then take all kinds of flour and bake a loaf as broad as a man's palm, and knead it with milk and holy water, and lay it under the first furrow. Then say:

Field filled with food, to feed mankind,
Blooming brightly, be you blessed,
In the holy name of He who made heaven, and earth on which we live, May the God who made these grounds grant to us his growing gifts That each kind of seed may come to good.

Then say three times, Crescite in nomine patris, sit benedicti. Amen and the Lord's Prayer three times

The Christian elements in the prayers themselves can be struck out, leaving wholly Heathen prayers without any damage to them. But this is not what we are looking at, what we are looking at is the general outline of the rite. The aim being to design an alternative outline one can use as a framework for other rites.

The beginning of the rite involves taking four turfs of earth from the field. You then mix, "yeast and milk from every cow that is in the land, and part of every kind of tree grown on the land, except hard beams, and part of every identifiable herb except the buckbean only, and add to them holy water." And you dip the turfs in this. One then has these blessed by a priest. Once this is done one creates four crosses of quickbeam, and place these in a pit with the turfs. Ignoring the obvious Christian actions, this part of the rite could be Heathen in origin. The laying of the quickbeams resemble the use of symbols to perform land takings outlined in the Icelandic Landnamabok

Þeir fóru til Íslands ok sigldu fyrir norðan landit ok vestr um Sléttu í fjörðinn. Þeir settu öxi í Reistargnúp ok kölluðu því Öxarfjörð. Þeir settu örn upp fyrir vestan ok kölluðu þar Arnarþúfu. En í þriðja stað settu þeir kross. Þar nefndu þeir Krossás. Svá helguðu þeir sér allan Öxarfjörð.

"They set an ax on Reistargnúp and called it Öxarfjörð. They set an eagle up in the west and called it Arnarþúfu. And the third they set a cross. They named it Krossás. So they hallowed all of Öxarfjörð.

The use of symbols at cardinal points of the land is seen in other mixed faiths context in the Landnamabok and some Icelandic sagas. The only time one sees the use of anything other than symbols in land taking is for temples (in which case fire was used). Therefore, the Christian who adapted the Heathen rite probably unknowingly included a rite for land taking within the Æcer Bót. The taking of land in the Icelandic corpus had religious overtones whether the land was used as a farm or a temple. Therefore, this portion of the rite is likely to be a way of making the land sacred to the Ése (Æsir) and Wen (Vanir).

One then turns counter clockwise three times, and then lays down flat on the ground invoking deities. The meaning of these actions are unknown, but probably are done in respect to the Gods and Goddesses. It is also likely they may simply be done for luck, or were a Christian substitute for dancing. Being prostate is perhaps a survival of rites mentioned by Taticus in regards to the Semnones. The Semnones would only enter a certain grove bound, and if they fell had to roll out of it. The Christian prayers said at this point are likely a subsitution for some form of Heathen prayers where one laid flat on the ground to pronounce them. The deities could have been Woden, Frea (Frey), and Frige (Frigga) or any variety of two Gods and a Goddess abased on the Christian combination here of Christ, God, and Mother Mary. More than likely these were short prayers inviting the Gods and Goddesses. Again this is speculation, as much of this study of the AElig;cer Bót is. Next comes the blessing of the plow with unknown seeds, followed by the Earth prayer. The plow is then driven forward and it is followed by another prayer. Bread or cakes (perhaps such as the cakes that were given to the Gods Goddesses Bede mentioned in reference to Solmonaþ, and perhaps of which the the cross buns eaten at Easter are a survival). This was followed by another prayer asking for fertility of the land and good crops.

With this information, we can formulate an outline that is quite unlike that of the blot seen in the *Heimskringla*. This faining is more suited to non-animal rites such as libations and the giving of bread and cakes. For the outline, one can probably dispense with many of the superstitious elements that may owe more to Christianity than Heathenry. One might outline it as below:

1) Preparation: In this portion of the rite outline, one prepares whatever they may need for the rite. Bake bread, prepare turfs such as in this rite, or obtain mead.

2) Blessing of gifts to be given: Here we are going to see part of the blot outline. Although holy water (water drawn from a spring, the dew, or brook before sunrise on a Spring morning) may be used instead of blood or mead. Most modern Heathens would probably prefer the use of mead. Just as in the blót the items would be blessed by sprinkling them with water or mead.

3) Creation of sacred space: One can then perform the Wéonde Song, Hammer Rite, or erect sacred symbols in order to make the land sacred.

4) Ritual Actions: One then turns counter clockwise three times and lays prostate on the ground, and says prayers to three deities. The content of these prayers is unknown, and the Christian substitutions give us no clues. The only possible clue they may give is these are prayers commonly used by Christians for protection. But more than likely they were an invite to the Gods and Goddesses.

5) The First Bede: This prayer is the first of the major two prayers of the rite. This bede if one follows the

Æcer Bót is a song of praise. The Goddess Earth is greeted (or rather her mother) with the traditional greeting of "wes hál" which generally would be followed by praise of the deity.

6) More Ritual Actions: As we are trying to create a general ritual action, one need not drive a plow through their yard. But one will need to dig a hole. This hole is where one will put the offering being given to the Gods.

7) The Second Bede: A shorter bede in praise of the Gods and Goddesses giving the gifts to them.

8)Offering: One pours the mead or places bread in the hole and follows this with a prayer asking for gifts from the Gods and Goddeses.

This outline is perhaps more versatile than the blót outline offered by Snorri in the *Heimskringla*. No doubt it had entirely different uses, and may have originally been a rite for blessing a plow instead of a charm for making land fruitful. That is was a "sacrifice" can be seen by the burial of bread or cakes at its end, just as Bede mentioned in his work De Temporum Ratione.

A Divination Faining

When most think of faining they think of
the standard outline taking from the *Heimskringla* or at
most the alternative form from the Æcer-Bót, but if
you seek through the lore, you can find other forms.
One such is found in the *Flateyjarbók*. According to H.
R. Eliis Davidson:

This is not the only account of a god carried around in a
wagon. Another story in *Flateyjarbók* (1, 4676) shows
the Swedish king himself consulting such a god, who is
here called Lýtir. Little is known of such a deity, but his
name seems to have inspired a number of Swedish
place-names, and it is possible that it was one of the
titles of Freyr. King Eric of Sweden is said to have led
the god's wagon to a certain place, and waited until it
became heavy, the sign that the god was present within.
Then the wagon was drawn to the king's hall, and Eric
greeted the god, drank a horn in his honour, and put
various questions to him. Here then the privalieged person consulting the god was the king himself, and some
kind of divination ceremony seems to have taken place.
(H.R. Ellis Davidson "Gods and Myths of Northern
Euorpe, p.p. 94-95)

This clue to a divination rite can be adapted to a
faining. For this one will need someone, preferably a
leader type (a kindred leader, head of household, or lord
of a theod) someone that knows spæ, a wéoh, and folks
that the wéoh can travel around to. Below is a rough
outline, based on the *Heimskringla* account as follows:

111

It was an old custom, that when there was to be sacrifice all the bondes should come to the spot where the temple stood and bring with them all that they required while the festival of the sacrifice lasted. To this festival all the men brought ale with them; and all kinds of cattle, as well as horses, were slaughtered, and all the blood that came from them was called "hlaut", and the vessels in which it was collected were called hlaut-vessels. Hlaut-staves were made, like sprinkling brushes, with which the whole of the altars and the temple walls, both outside and inside, were sprinkled over, and also the people were sprinkled with the blood; but the flesh was boiled into savoury meat for those present. The fire was in the middle of the floor of the temple, and over it hung the kettles, and the full goblets were handed across the fire; and he who made the feast, and was a chief, blessed the full goblets, and all the meat of the sacrifice. And first Odin's goblet was emptied for victory and power to his king; thereafter, Niord's and Frey's goblets for peace and a good season. Then it was the custom of many to empty the brage-goblet; and then the guests emptied a goblet to the memory of departed friends, called the remembrance goblet.

From this account an outline can be made, with the additional elements from the Flateyjarbók.

Items Needed:

horn

blot bowl

mead

runes

hlaut-teinn

a wéoh

1) Sensing the sacred: In the Flateyjar-bók account we are told the procession began when the idol felt "heavy." Now whether this meant the wéoh was literally heavy, or merely that there was a sacred presence we do not know. In Germania, the Nerthus account says it was when the goddess was present. No other procession accounts are helpful. Therefore, one can use their intuition as a guide as to weather or not the deity is present.

2) The procession: It is unlikely one has a sacred cart, or the ability to transport it from place to place if they did. Therefore, a car will have to do. One should make sure the wéoh stops at every member's household, and that while there, they make offerings and prayers to it. When the time is right, i.e. faining day, the wéoh should be brought to the house of the person performing the faining.

3) Hallowing the mead: At this point, one is ready to begin the rite its self. To start the rite, one should hallow the mead by passing it over a fire (a candle will do), and blessing it with the words, "Þunor wéoh," or "Thor make sacred."

4) Reading the runes: Accounts outside the *Heimskringla* indicate that rune readings were done to see if the auspices were good for a faining. One should put all 24 or 33 runes into the blot bowl and then draw out three. The priest should then interpret the reading, and announce whether or not things are favorable.

5) Sprinkling or blessing the temple and folk: The temple walls, altar, and folk were then sprinkled or blessed by the priests. This act is also mentioned in Eyrbygja

Saga in the description of Thorolf Mostrarskeggy's hof.

6) Drinking the full: At this point, the leader of the group drinks to the deity of the wéoh. This should be worded as a standard prayer. Prayers or bedes generally followed the following outline: a) A "wassailing" of the god or Gods, a prime example being the one in the Sigdrífumál which opens with "Hail to thee Dæg, hail ye Dæg's sons" and proceeds to "wassail" the Gods. b) A boast of the god or Gods' great deeds. c) A petition or request.

7) The "conversation": At this point the spæman, should kneel by the wéoh and he or she should be ready to "channel" or interpret the responses of the deity. Once ready the leader then asks questions of the wéoh, being careful to direct the questions to the wéoh and not the spæman. Information on how the spæman can operate can be found in my book Germanic Magic or on the Miercinga Theod website (http://www.ealdriht.org).

8) The fulls: Once the conversation is over, other members of the group may make toasts to the deity.

9) The gifting: The mead is then poured in the blot bowl, and offered to the wéoh with words of thanks.

As can be seen this rite does not stray far from the standard worship outline for a libation. It can be adapted to blot by Theodsmen, or other forms of fainings. As this rite has not been done in a thousand or so years, it may be hit and miss at first, but given time, Heathens will be able to bring back to life a rite of old.

Wóden Worhte Wéos:
Idols in Germanic Heathenry

Introduction

Every religion has something or someplace where people go to feel the numinous presence of its deities. Christians attend churches, Hindus kneel at images of their deities, and Jews read in synagogue. In this sense, a Protestant church is no different than a Hindu temple, both use sacred objects or places as focal points for worship. The ancient Germanic tribes were no different. From the earliest literature about them in the Roman accounts to the Icelandic Sagas, we have over one thousand years of Heathen worship involving groves, temples, and wéos or idols. The Old English word, wéoh is related to other words meaning sacred. Old Norse, vé meant "sacred space" or "a place to worship," (there are indications the Old English word carried these connotations as well), while modern German weih as in Weihnachten or "Christmas time" means "sacred." For that reason it will be used throughout this work for the most part in preference to the Old French idol, which conjures up images of Middle Easterners worshiping graven images thought to be the deity incarnate.

Sacred Presence

Ancient Heathen uses of wéos is fundamentally different from what modern culture views idolatry to be. The wéoh was not the deity its self, but the focus of

116

the deity's power out to the deity's followers, and the focus of the follower's worship back to the deity. It was not the deity incarnate, so much as a conduit for the numinous power of the deity. In Heathen terms, the *mægen* or hamingja of the deity was present and being given to the folk, while the folk's *mægen* or hamingja would flow the other way. This can be seen in part in the earliest accounts such as the tale of Nerthus in Germania:

There is nothing particularly noteworthy about these people in detail, but they are distinguished by a common worship of Nerthus, or Mother Earth. They believe that she interests herself in human affairs and rides through their peoples. In an island of Ocean stands a sacred grove, and in the grove stands a car draped with a cloth which none but the priest may touch. The priest can feel the presence of the goddess in this holy of holies, and attends her, in deepest reverence, as her car is drawn by kine.

The Latin reads not much differently, but what is important to note here is the priest must sense the presence of Nerthus. This indicates she is not always present in the we'oh, and therefore is not thought to be the we'oh. This stands in stark contrast to modern Christian views on "idol worship," where it is assumed that the idol is the deity. The idol is no more the deity than the Bible is the Christian god. Later literature indicates that Germanic peoples saw a link between the we'oh, and the deity. In a very biased account, in Olaf's Saga, King Olaf encounters a we'oh of Thor being carried:

On the next day, as it chanced, there was no rain, and when the people were all gathered together in the early dawn Bishop Sigurd rose in his gown, with a mitre on his head and a crozier in his hand, and preached to the peasants and told them many tokens which God had shown. And presently King Olaf saw a crowd of men approaching, carrying a large image, ornamented all over with gold and silver. The people all stood up and bowed to the monster, which was placed in the middle of the meeting place.

"Where is your God now, O king?" cried Gudbrand, rising and addressing Olaf. "It seems to me that your boasting, and that of the horned man, whom you call your bishop, is far less than yesterday. It is because our god, who rules all, has come, and looks on you with keen eyes. And I see that you are full of terror at sight of him! Now throw off this new superstition of yours — this belief in a God who cannot be seen — and acknowledge the greatness of Thor!"

It is apparent that the followers of Thor here felt their deity to be present in the wéoh, though the author of the account may have misunderstood exactly what the followers thought was present. Another late tale about an idol of Frey is perhaps an even more twisted version of a deity's presence in a wéoh. In the Flateyjarbók,Gunnarr Helming posed as the God after having wrestled with a wéoh of Frey.

Wéos of Bronze and Wood

The earliest wéohas seem to have been made of wood. Luckily, thanks to the bogs of Denmark, a few examples have survived as well as a few in other places such as Oldenburg. They are roughly carved limbs of trees dated to about 400 BCE to 100 CE. One in particular is famous, the Broddenbjerg God, having been dug out of a bog, and potentially (judging by its phallus) to be the god Fréa (Frey). This habit of making wéos out of wood is reflected in an Old Norse word, "skurdhgodhdyrkari 'idolater,' literally translated as 'one who cultivates carved gods'" (Gundarsson) Other words also indicated that the wéos were made of wood such as Old Norse trégudh and holzgott both mean "tree god." This link to wood is important, while the ancient Germanic peoples were no experts with stone, they were with metal, and yet, all idols from the earliest periods are of wood. Metal ones are not seen until later. This is important. We are told in the Maxims I that Wóden worhte wéos. The first thought about this line, is that Woden made idols, thus Woden was the God of idolatry. No doubt that is what the Christian transcriptionist thought. However, this may have been a legitimate Heathen phrase. In the Elder Edda, in the Voluspa we are told that Odin gave elm and ash "form." And in the Havamal, we are told by Odin, "my garments once I gave in the field to two tree men; heroes they seemed when once they were clothed; 'tis the naked who suffer shame!" Man was made out of trees, and Woden could give trees life. Thus, wood made the ideal medium for a conduit to and from the Ése and Wen. In that sense, Woden did make wéos. The earliest metal wéos date to the Bronze Age, but are much smaller, and would seem to have been for personal use. These do not become common, judging by finds until late in the Viking Age.

The Procession of Wéos

Medieval processions of saints are common enough in the memory of modern man. What is not commonly known is there is plenty of evidence this practice goes back to the Heathen period when wéoas were carried about. The earliest reference is that of Nerthus, and the one of Thor above also serves as an example, as is the tale in the Flateyjarbók. Instances such as these are not limited to Denmark and the rest of Scandinavia. There is an example amongst the Goths drawing a cart about to Christians.

It is said that a wooden image was placed on a wagon, and that those instructed by Athanaric to undertake this task wheeled it round to the tent of any of those who were denounced as Christians and ordered them to do homage and sacrifice to it; and the tents of those who refused to do so were burned, with the people inside. (Heather)

Wéos in Divination

There is a unique case in the Flateyjarbók of an idol being used in a divination ceremony. A wéoh named Lýtir is lead around the kingdom until finally it is brought before the king who questions it. Just as in the Nerthus account, the priest waits until they feel the presence of the God, characterized as being when the wéoh is heavy. Then it is lead around the land coming to rest at the hall of the Swedish king. The king then consults the wéoh. The name of the God appears to mean "enlightening," perhaps coming from Old Norse lýsa, "to light up," although some hold it as coming from lýta, "to blemish."

Wéos in the Temple

There are numerous mentions of wéoes in temple worship. We know from Bede that they existed in what was to be England:

.....and when he inquired who should profane the alters and temples of idols with the enclosures that were about them, the high priest answered, "I, for who can more properly than myself destroy those things which I worshiped through ignorance...."

We also know that wéos received libations from Adam of Bremen:

If plague and famine threatens, a libation is poured to the idol Thor; if war, to Odin; if marriages are to be celebrated, to Frey.

Usually, one thinks of larger versions of the small metal idols we see from the later Viking Age made in metal or stone. However, these wéos may have been of wood. We are told in the Eyrbyggja Saga that Thorolf threw his high seat pillars overboard to see where to land. These pillars had "god nails" in them perhaps for the striking of sparks mimicking lightning. (Davidson)

Wéos at War

Wéos were not reserved for just the temple and worship. They also went to war according to Germania

Nor when the Priests do this, is the same considered as a punishment, or arising from the orders of the general, but from the immediate command of the Deity, Him whom they believe to accompany them in war. They therefore carry with them when going to fight, certain images and figures taken out of their holy groves.

This practice seems to have stopped by the Viking era or they neglected to speak of it. Never the less, the idea behind the carrying of wéos into war is pretty obvious. The deities were expected to help with the outcome of the battle. In many ways the practice was probably similar to that of the Crusaders carrying the true cross into battle figuring they could never be defeated as long as they had it. Woden, being the god of vicotry was probably the favored deity for this, but no doubt other wéos such as Tiw (Tyr) may have been carried also.

The Creation of Wéos

The ancient Heathens no doubt carved their wéos out of whatever wood they felt the Gods guided them to. Modern Heathen practice however, has not made much use of wooden idols. Largely, this is because most do not have space for a large log in their backyard, nor the time to carve it. None the less, one can make smaller representations that can rest on their home altar. First one must find the right kind of wood. One may use the lore as a guide, using oak or rowan for Þunor (Thor), or maple for Fréo (Freya) for example. Or one may just follow "gut feeling." Some considerations are to be made though. A hard wood takes better to sanding than carving, and brittle woods cannot be easily engraved with an engraving bit on a Dremel. Your choice of tools will determine largely what kind of wood one will use. Some woods do well with whittling, others better with sanding. Soft woods do not do well with burning. Once you have decided what kind of wood to use, one can then settle on a design. Many do this by simple freehand, letting the form take shape as they carve. Others find it better to carve a rough outline on the wood. Use whatever works best for you.

As to what form of tool you use, there are a variety. Sanding or engraving bits with a Dremel work well. One can use a pocket knife or exacto-knife to carve, or even use a wood burner to create their wéoh. Experiment and find what is best for you. Of course, once you carve your wéos, you will want to start using them in fainings, making sure to bless them. And maybe someday, you will feel the presence of the Gods and Goddesses in them.

Mothers' Night: The Start of a New Year

The Evidence

Incipiebant autem annum ab ocatavo kelendarum ianuariarum die, ubi nunc natalem domini celebramus. Et ipasm noctem nunc nobis sacrosanctam, tunc gentili vocabulo modranect, id est matrum noctem, appellabant, ob causam, ut suspicamur, ceremoniarum quas in ea pervigiles agebant.

They began the year with December 25, the day we now celebrate as Christmas; and the very night to which we attach special sanctity they designated by the heathen term módraniht, that is, the mothers' night --- a name bestowed, I suspect, on account of the ceremonies they performed while watching this night through. (Charles W, Jones translation)

Evidence of Módraniht or Mothers' Night remains illusive. Bede is the only one to mention it. No other Anglo-Saxon source mentions it. Yet we are fortunate that we have a similar set of rites mentioned in other Germanic sources. In the Icelandic Sagas there is frequently mentioned the Dísablót. Most sources have Dísablót as taking place at Winter Nights, the last two days of Fall and first day of Winter in the Icelandic calendar. Winter Nights or Veturnætur was the start of the New Year in Iceland, just as Mothers Night was for the

Anglo-Saxons. In some way, the ancient Germanic peoples may have felt that the New Year was somehow sacred to the ancestral mothers. Why? We can only speculate. It may be that they saw it as the birth of the New Year, or that the ancestral women were seen as guarding the home, and therefore called on during the harsh winter months.

This link between Goddesses and the New Year is apparently not limited to the Anglo-Saxons and Norse. A perusal of Grimm's Teutonic Mythology shows that the Yule tide was sacred in someway to several Goddesses. Among them were Peratha:

> *It still remains for us to explain her precise connexion with a particular day of the year. It is either on Dec. 25 (dies natalis), or twelve days after Christmas, on Jan. 6, when the star appeared to the Three Kings (magi), that the christian church celebrates the feast of the manifestation of Christ under the name of epiphania (v. Ducange, sub v.), bethphania or theophania (O. Fr. tiephaine, tiphagne). In an OHG. gloss (Emm. 394), theophania is rendered giperahta naht, the bright night of the heavenly vision that appeared to the shepherds in the field. Documents of the Mid. Ages give dates in the dative case: 'perchtentag, perhtennaht' (for OHG. zi demo perahtin taga, zi deru Perahtûn naht); again, 'an der berechtnaht,' M. Beham*

(Mone, anz. 4, 451); 'ze perhnahten,'
MB. 8, 540 (an. 1302); 'unze an den ah-
todin tac nâh der Perhtage,' till the
eighth day after the Perht's (fem.) day,
Fundgr. 110, 22; 'von dem nehsten
Berhtag,' MB. 9, 138 (an. 1317); 'an
dem Prehentag,' MB. 7, 256 (an. 1349);-
--these and other contracted forms are
cited with references in Scheffer's Hal-
taus p. 75, and Schm. 1, 194. Now from
this there might very easily grow up a
personification, Perchtentac, Perchten-
naht, the bright day becoming Bright's,
i.e., dame Bright's, day. (Conrad of
Dankrotsheim, p. 123, puts his milde
Behte down a week earlier, on Dec. 30.)
(Stallybrass (tr.) . Grimm, Teutonic My-
thology, Chapter 13)

It is easy to note here that the days given as being in connection with her are Dec. 25, the old date under the Julian calendar for Mothers Night, or Twelfth
Night, on or around New Year's Day under the Gregorian calendar. Both could point to the Goddess being
linked to the start of the New Year. Yule is also sacred
to Holda:

Her annual progress, which like those of Herke
and Berhta, is made to fall between Christmas and
Twelfth-day, when the supernatural has sway and wild
beasts like the wolf are not mentioned by their names,
brings fertility to the land. Not otherwise does 'Derk
with the boar,' that Freyr of the Netherlands (p. 214),

appear to go his rounds and look after the ploughs. At the same time Holda, like Wuotan, can also ride on the winds, clothed in terror, and she, like the god, belongs to the 'wutende heer.' From this arose the fancy, that witches ride in Holla's company (ch. XXXIV, snow-wives); it was already known to Burchard, and now in Upper Hesse and the Westerwald, Holle-riding, to ride with Holle, is equivalent to a witches' ride. (Stallybrass (tr.), Grimm, Teutonic Mythology, Chapter 13, page 5)

Other Goddess such as Beratha and Herke are also seen as holding Yule as a sacred season:

> In the Mark she is called frau Harke, and is said to fly through the country between Christmas and Twelfth-day, dispensing earthly goods in abundance; by Epiphany the maids have to finish spinning their flax, else frau Harke gives them a good scratching or soils their distaff. (Stallybrass (tr.), Grimm, Teutonic Mythology, Chapter 13, page 1)

With Berahta we have also to consider Holda, Diana and Herodias. Berahta and Holda shew themselves, like frau Gaude (p. 925), in the 'twelves' about New-year's day.(Stallybrass (tr.), Grimm, Teutonic Mythology, Chapter 31, page 4)

There is, therefore, circumstantial evidence for some sort of rite linked to the Goddesses at the start of the New Year amongst the Germanic peoples in what is now Germany. For there not to be some form of rite linked to the above named Goddesses in connection with Yule would seem highly unusual.

The Rites

Unfortunately, we have little to no evidence of what rites were performed. We can surmise from the German folk tales that all work was put away during the Twelve Nights. Again and again in folk tales about Holda and Peratha we here that women are not to spin during Yule, that farm implements must be put away, in essence all work for the year must be done. Beyond that, we must go farther abroad for information. Along Hadrian's Wall, in Germany, northern Italy, and modern France there are found altars that were part of the Matron Cult, or Cult of Mothers. Many of these bear Germanic names, although some names are in Latin, and others Gaulish.

More than simple votive stones have been found, however: in some areas there were large cult centers, temples and monuments, especially along the Rhine. Some of the largest were in Pesch, Nettersheim, and Bonn. The temples, monuments and votive stones show that the following were important to the worship of the mothers:
-burning bowls of incense
-sacrifices of fruit, fish, and pigs,
-imagery of fruit baskets, plants, trees, babies, children, cloths for wrapping babies, and snakes.

Images of the mothers generally show them in a group

of three, though occasionally two or one are found; usually at least one of them holds a basket of fruit, and often a baby is held. Often all of them have clothing and hairstyles or head dressing indicating their matron status, though sometimes the middle figure is shown dressed as a maiden, with her hair loose. (Winifred Hodge, Matrons and Disisr: The Heathen Tribal Mothers retrieved from http://www.friggasweb.org/matrons.html on Dec. 4 20006 CE).

These Goddesses are given names that relate to "giving" such as Gabiae, Friagabiae, and Alagabiae. From this we can surmise that perhaps the rites consisted of asking the Goddesses for prosperity, gifts for the coming new year. The gifts given the Goddesses would have consisted of bowls of incense, gifts of fruit, grain, and perhaps even the sacrifice of swine.

The Icelandic sagas give us a little more information. In Egil's Saga, we are told a great feast was held followed by the drinking of many horns of ale (in essence, a symbel). Many became drunk to the point of being sick, and the night ended in the death of Bard at Egil's hands. We are told not much more than that. Víga-Glúms Saga presents a similar picture. In Hervarar Saga, the rites were done outdoors at night, and Alfhild, the king's daughter, reddened the altar with blood. Unfortunately, again we are not told much more than that. We can however, figure out from this that both faining and symbel were held, and from the evidence of the cult of Matrons what forms the gifts may have taken.

Conclusion

Using the above information, Mothers' Night can be filled out to include the activities of faining and symbel. We know from the evidence provided by the Matron Cult of the late Roman Empire that incense was burned, and from Norse accounts that some form of animal sacrifice may have taken place. There was more than likely following the faining, a feast, followed by symbel. And all this took place at night with worship taking place outside, but with symbel and feast inside. Bede implies that the rites may have taken the whole of the night, as do the Norse sources. This would have opened the 12 Nights of Yule, but the goddesses were not forgotten after that night. For the rest of the 12 nights certain restrictions applied such as the putting away of work tools and not laboring. If these restrictions were not obeyed, the wrath of the Goddesses could be expected.

Englisc Rímbóc The Anglo-Saxon Calendar

Bede's Account of the Calendar in *De Temporum Ratione*

One of the least studied things in ancient Anglo-Saxon culture is the old pagan calendar. Yet, it is an area of most interest for many. What we know of the calendar was handed down to us by Bede in his work *De Temporum Ratione*. Unfortunately, while Bede gave us much information, he also left us in quite a mystery about how the calendar worked. We know not from his information alone whether the months were reckoned by the phases of the moon, and if so, whether they began on the Full or New Moon. We are perplexed how a fixed solar date could be the start of the year in a calendar that appears to be solar lunar (a calendar using both the Sun to keep track of years and the Moon to keep track of months), and even more so by when that fixed date occurs. Still, the information Bede gave us, along with other clues from Anglo-Saxon culture, the practices of other cultures, and comparison with the Icelandic calendar can result in a reliable reconstruction.

Bede begins his account of the old Heathen calendar by saying

Antiqui autem anglorum populi (neque enim mihi congrum videtur aliarum gentium annalem observantiam dicere et meæ reticere) iutxa cursum lunæ suos menses computavere. Unde et a luna hebræorum et græcorum more nomen accipiuiunt; siduidem apud eos luna mona, mensis appellatur monath.

The ancient English peoples -- for it does not seem to me proper to explain the yearly observance of other nations, and to keep silence concerning my own -- reckoned their months by the course of the moon, just as they were named from the moon in Hebrew and Greek. (Charles W, Jones translation)

Thus the mystery begins from the start of his text. Most have thought that "cursum lunæ suos menses computavere (by the course of the moon calculated)" indicates that the months were determined by the phases of the Moon. However, besides keeping track of time through the phases of the Moon, one can also keep track of time by the path the Moon takes through the sky. Using the course of the Moon to keep track of time results in using what modern astronomers call a sideral month, which is 27 days 7 hours and 43 minutes long. Every 27 days the moon returns to the same position in the sky it was 27 days before. The scholar Vaster Guðmundsson believed that this was the form of month the Norse used, and used it in his theoretical reconstruction of the ancient Scandinavian calendar (Guðmundsson. 1924, p.88). It is possible then that the Anglo-Saxons also did the same. However, as Bede draws a comparison to the Greek and Hebrew calendars, we may want to assume that the Anglo-Saxons used a synodic month (a month measured from a phase of the Moon to the next time that phase of the Moon occurs). There are other clues in Bede's account, that indicate this was so, and I will touch on those later. Bede then goes on to name the months of the old Anglo-Saxon calendar and further gives the corresponding Roman month.

Primusqu eorum mesis, quem latini ianuarium vocant, dicitur giuli; deinde februarius, solmonah; martius, hredmonath; aprilis, eosturmonath; maius, thrimilchi; iunius lida; iulius, similiter lida; augustus, vveodmonath; september, halegmonath; october, vvinterfilleth; november, blodmonath; december, giuli eodem quo ianuarius nomine vocatur.

The first month, which the Romans name January, is with them *Giuli.* Then follow February, *Solmónaþ*; *March, Hrédmónaþ*; April, *Éosturmónaþ*; May, *Þrimilchi;* June, *Lípa;* July also *Lípa;* August, *Wéodmónaþ; September, Háligmónaþ;* October, *Winterfylleþ;* November, *Blótmónaþ;* Decemeber, *Giuuli,* the same as for January. (Charles W, Jones translation)

At first this may not seem important, however, it shows that the Anglo-Saxon months roughly followed the Roman ones, enough so that Bede could draw correspondences. This shows what we have suspected, that the calendar was a solar lunar one, not a straight lunar calendar. And while it does not rule out the use of the sideral month, it increases the odds that the Anglo-Saxons used a synodic month. Sideral months being shorter would move more within the solar year. Synodic months being closer in length to the Roman fixed months would make for a closer comparison, and not move as much in relation to the seasons as long as intercalary (leap) months were used.

Bede then touches on when the year started. Something he has already hinted at by naming *Giuli,* the month corresponding to January as the first month.

Incipiebant autem annum ab ocatavo kelendarum ianuariarum die, ubi nunc natalem domini celebramus. Et ipasm noctem nunc nobis sacrosanctam, tunc gentili vocabulo modranect, id est matrum noctem, appellabant, ob causam, ut suspicamur, ceremoniarum quas in ea pervigiles agebant.

"They began the year with December 25, the day we now celebrate as Christmas; and the very night to which we attach special sanctity they designated by the heathen term *módraniht,* that is, the mothers' night --- a name bestowed, I suspect, on account of the ceremonies they performed while watching this night through. (Charles W, Jones translation)

At that time, under the old Julian calendar, December 25 (or eight days before the calends of January as Bede puts it) was also the winter solstice. The problem with this is that if the Anglo-Saxon calendar was a solar lunar calendar, then it could not have a starting point that was a fixed solar date (at least not have such a fixed date and operate with any accuracy). Bede may have confused an Anglo-Saxon pagan mid-winter festival with a New Year's celebration. Or it is possible the actual start of the new year was on the Full or New Moon near the solstice. It is also possible the Anglo-Saxons used a sideral month and somehow managed to reconcile its differences with the solar year (though it would be as difficult to do this as reconciling the start of a lunar calendar using synodic months in such a fashion). Finally, the most distinct possibility perhaps is the Anglo-Saxon Heathens used more than one calendar for more than one purpose. That is they could have used a solar calendar separate from the one Bede presented, and it was the solar calendar whose new year began on December 25. There have been many theories as to why the year began on December 25, ranging from Roman borrowing to influences of Mithraism, but few have thought it the start of a separate calendar. The possibility is distinct however.

The Icelanders, for example, did use a solar calendar which they established in 930 CE in conjunction with the Norse lunar months (which ceased to be lunar), but reformed again in 955. The core of this calendar consisted of two seasons, winter and summer for a year of 364 days or 52 weeks. Each season was 26 weeks long. To this calendar was added one week every seven years as a "leap week," to keep it in line with the solar year (much as a day is added every four years to the Gregorian calendar today). New Year's Day was Veturnætur or "Winter Nights," a time near the Fall equinox. While some scholars have attributed the Icelanders adopting a solar calendar as being due to Classical and Christian influence (via trade relations with the then Christian Anglo-Saxons and Irish), one cannot rule out the possibility a solar calendar was a native idea to most Germanic peoples. The Anglo-Saxons like the Icelanders also had only two seasons, Summer and Winter, and this is even stated by Bede (though elsewhere he refers to four, a comment that can be attributed to his Church education which held there were four seasons, not two). It would not be surprising then if they used a separate solar calendar based on the equinoxes and solstices, perhaps even using weeks for time reckoning much like the Icelanders did. Further it would not be far fetched if they saw Módranect as some sort of marker in this calendar. In Bede's account the start of the year, he notes the start of Winter (while linked to a Full Moon, it would be close to what we

135

know as autumn), the Winter solstice, and the fact months were added after the Summer solstice. It would be difficult therefore to assume that the Anglo-Saxons and Germanic peoples in general could not have kept track of time by the Sun. Bede then goes on to talk about the use of an intercalary month called Þriliða.

cum vero temporibus, hoc est xiii mensium lunarium, annus occurreret, superfluum mensem æstati apponebant, ita ut tunc tres menses simul lida nomine vocarentur, et ob id annus ille thrilidi cognominabatur habens quattuor menses æstatis, ternos ut semper temporum cæsterorum.

When, however, an embolism occurred, that is, a year of thirteen lunar months, they added the intercalated month to the summer, so that in that case three months in succession were called *Líþa.* Such a year was known as *Þrilíþi,* having four months of summer, and three of the other seasons. (Charles W, Jones translation)

We know from this statement by Bede that *Þriliða* was added in some years in the Summer to bring the calendar back in line with the solar cycle. This again is a clue that the calendar was indeed a solar lunar one, most likely using synodic months (using one phase of the Moon to its next occurrence as a way of measuring a month). The Chinese, Hebrews, and even the ancient Romans used similar methods to adjust their calendars.

Item principaliter annum totem in duo tempora, hiemis videlicet et æstatis, dispertiebant - sex illos menses quibus longiores sunt noctinus dies æstati tribuendo, sex reliquos hiemi. Unde et mensem quo hiemalia tempora incipiebant vvinterfilleth apbellabant, composito nomine ab jieme et plenilunio quia videlicet a plenilunio eiusdem mensis hiems sortiretur initium.

The general division of the year was into two seasons, winter and summer, summer comprising the six months in which the days are longer than the nights, and winter the others. Hence the month with which they began the winter season was called *Winterfylleþ,* a name compounded of the terms for winter and full moon, because from the full moon of that month winter was esteemed to begin. (Charles W, Jones translation)

It is worth noting that the time of *Winterfylleþ* was also the time the Old Norse started their year (Veturnætur or "Winter Nights"), and there has been speculation on whether or not the actual new year of the calendar presented by Bede did not start at this time also, that Bede was mistaken. That Winter could be used of the entire year and not just the season is apparent to anyone that has studied Old English. The Anglo-Saxons counted years by winters and even had such terms as *wintergetel* "a number of years" and *winter-steal* "a one year old stallion." Garman Lord in *The Way of the Heathen* even theorizes that perhaps the name *Winterfylleþ* could have meant something closer to "New Year's Day." More important though, what Bede has to say about *Winterfylleþ* is also a clue that the months began with the Full Moon. Bede goes on to discuss the meaning of the month names, and as such this is his extent of clues on how the calendar operated. For more information on exactly how the calendar worked we must go outside his text to Anglo-Saxon concepts of the day, as well as draw from other cultures with solar lunar calendars.

137

One of the primary problems with the calendar is determining when the months began. Since few ancient cultures used the sideral month in calendars of this type, we can safely assume perhaps that the ancient Angles, Saxons, and Jutes used a synodic month like the Chinese, Hebrews, ancient Romans, and most other peoples in the world. But then we are faced with the question of when did the months begin? The only clue Bede gives us is in the name of *Winterfylleþ,* when he states that Winter was said to start from the Full Moon of that month. If Winter started on the Full Moon of *Winterfylleþ* and each season only had six months (not portions of months but whole months) then we almost must assume that *Winterfylleþ* began on the Full Moon. Then again Bede states Winter began on the Full Moon of that month, meaning that the month its self might not begin on the Full Moon. For a solution to this dilemma we must look to other cultures with similar ways of seeing tides as well as closely related cultures.

A bronze plaque with a calendar used by the Gauls engraved on it was found in Coligny, France, in 1897, and dated to about 50 CE. This calendar consisted of 12 months with names of Celtic origin. Further these months began on the Full Moon. The Gauls had lived in close proximity to the Germanic peoples for centuries. At one point it is possible that some of the Germanic tribes had developed a fascination with Celtic culture (or alternately been subjugated by a Celtic people). Within the Germanic languages there are several Celtic borrowings of great antiquity. These borrowings were words for rulership and warfare. Among them are the modern English word iron, Old English *ríce,* "kingdom;" and Old English *ambeht,* "servant." It is possible then that due to Celtic influence the Anglo-Saxons used the Full Moon as the marker for the start of a new month. Most societies that use a solar lunar calendar however do not use the Full Moon as a starting point for months.

Indeed, there is just as much evidence when we look at other cultures for the Anglo-Saxon calendar beginning its months on the first crescent of the New Moon. Further the evidence is also more convincing when common sense is applied. The first and best argument is that it is difficult to determine precisely when the Full Moon is occurring in Northern Europe. Indeed, it can appear to be full for three days, when in truth, only one of these days is the Full Moon. The New Moon can be almost as difficult to determine, but not quite as difficult. One can always look to the First Crescent of the New Moon, something easy to spot if one is watching for it, and not easily mistakened for another phase. This is precisely the moon phase many cultures such as the Hebrew and Babylonian cultures used. Further, cultures that start their day at sunset, also usually begin their year in the Winter months and their months (if they use a solar lunar calendar) with the New Moon or the First Crescent. The ancient Roman calendar prior to revisions by the Republic also started its months with the First Crescent as did that of the ancient Greek cultures. Perhaps the best evidence arguing for the Anglo-Saxons using the First Crescent is that of the Lithuanian calendar. The Lithuanian calendar not only started its months on the First Crescent of the New Moon, but also had a midwinter celebration the same time as Yule. Oddly enough though it started its year in April (Straižys and Klimka). Perhaps of all Indo-

European peoples the Balts have the most in common with the Germanic. Even their religion is very close to the ancient Germanic one with components such as a World Tree, and deities similar to our own such as the thunder god Perkunas who is not a far cry from the ever familiar Þunor (Thor), not to mention a Sun goddess and Moon god. Unfortunately, especially since it may be the closest comparison to the Anglo-Saxon calendar, not much has been written on the Lithuanian calendar in English. Yet considering the close relationship of the Balts to the Germanic peoples, it presents a good argument for the Anglo-Saxon months starting with the First Crescent, and not the Full Moon.

Another clue to the months starting on the First Crescent is when the Anglo-Saxons began their day. Other cultures such as the Hebrew that use the First Crescent as the starting point for their months, start their day at sunset (the Lithuanians seem to be an exception). We find this too with the Anglo-Saxons. Wódenesniht to an ancient Engle was not Wednesday night but Tuesday night; Wednesday began on what we would think of as Tuesday evening. We can also see this start of the day at Sunset with the festivals, for example, Módraniht mentioned by Bede. Modern survivals of this include Halloween (a contraction of "All Hallows Evening"), New Years Eve, and Walpurgis Night. The Old English word *niht*, not *dæg* was used for counting, that is one would say "10 nihtas" not "10 dægas" (a modern survival of this is our term fortnight). This too was indicative of cultures that started their months on the First Crescent. We can therefore probably safely assume therefore that the Anglo-Saxons used the First Crescent as a marker for the start of a month, although we can never be one hundred per cent certain (barring finding a lost document dating from the period detailing such calendar information).

Other Potential Calendars

As mentioned above, a solar lunar calendar may not have been the only way that the Anglo-Saxons kept track of times longer than a day. There were the two seasons called *missera* in Old English. We know that they had two seasons, but we do not know if they were used in such a way as the Icelanders later did. For the Icelanders, the *missera* played a more important role than the solar year. Indeed, their calendar was not based so much on the solar year as it was the half year. As detailed above, their calendar consisted of the two seasons, numbered 26 weeks each. The two seasons were further broken down into weeks. The week has always been a problematic time unit however. Most scholars view it as a borrowing from the Romans, who in turn borrowed it from the Greeks. Ultimately it is seen as having come from the Semitic cultures of the Middle East with its sole purpose being religious. That is scholars feel the week is a manmade time unit with no bearing on astronomical or natural events (unlike the month, the year, the day). The problem is that within the written record of many peoples such as the Celts and Germanics, there is no sign of there not being a 7 day week, or at least a week of some sort. So while scholars can claim that the week is a borrowing, they cannot prove definitively it is a borrowing. This problem is further complicated when one looks at how a week can be used in time keeping. The synodic month is approximately 29 days and 12 hours long. Four seven day weeks could then be used as a rough division of the month (being only a day or so off). This is somewhat confirmed by the origins of the word week which scholars think comes from an Indo-European word meaning "to turn." In other words, the word week might have originally referred to the turning of the phases of the moon (and it also may have been a longer time unit than now). Even there we are on shaky ground as while some consider it a native Germanic term, others see it as coming from Latin *vices* "recurrences."

While the week as we know it now may be a borrowing, the concept of a unit of time lasting several days (but only a fraction of a month) may not be. The Lithuanians used a nine day week at one point, which makes for a good division of the the sideral month. As mentioned above a sideral month, is 27 days 7 hours and 43 minutes long. Therefore the week in some form may have always been a Germanic time keeping unit (however, it may not have always been seven days long). Vaster Guðmundsson believed that the Norse used a five day week prior to the borrowing of the seven day week, and used this in his reconstruction of the Norse calendar. However, his week has no bearing on astronomical events either. The solar year is more evenly divided by five week periods though, and there is an Old Norse legal term referring to such a five day period as a *fimmt*. There could no doubt be other time units similar to the week we do not know of that the ancient Germanic peoples, and thus the ancient Angles, Saxons, and Jutes may have used. That information though is unfortunately lost if it ever existed.

Regardless, that they could have used a solar calendar similar to the Icelandic one after Roman contact is a certainty. They would have had the time unit of the week, and had all the astronomical knowledge to use one (which they had well before Roman contact). It could well be that such a solar calendar is seen lurking behind the solar lunar one as presented by Bede. He does after all refer to solar events such as the start of the year on the winter solstice and the seasons in his description of the calendar. The only problem is, we can keep on saying "could," as there is no evidence truly for or against the Anglo-Saxons using a solely solar calendar like that of the Icelanders. What we do know is that *missrera* could also be used to mean years, as its Old Norse cognate *missari* could also. Indeed, the Norse did not even truly have a term for the whole year. If the *missrera* then played a more important part in Anglo-Saxon time keeping, they would most certainly had a solar calendar as well.

Other Methods of Telling Time Shorter than a Day

On quite firmer ground than the possible use of a solar calendar is how the Anglo-Saxons divided the day. It would appear that they, like their Norse cousins divided the day into eight even divisions, or *stundas* (sometimes referred to as a *tíd* in Old English). Early Anglo-Saxon sundials (a *sol-merca* or *dægmæl*) show only four evenly spaced marks for telling time during daylight (these four divisions of daylight are paralleled by four at night). The names of these eight divisions are seen throughout Old English literature. They are: *úht* (roughly 3 am to 6 am), *morgen* (roughly 6 am to 9 am), *undern* (roughly 9 am to noon), *middæg* (roughly noon to 3 pm), *gelotendæg* (roughly 3 pm to 6 pm), *æfen* (roughly 6 pm to 9 pm), *niht* (roughly 9 pm to midnight), and *midniht* (roughly midnight to 3 am). Our usage of such words as morning, noon, and evening to divide up the day are but vestiges of this time keeping method. There is a very good article on how the Norse used these divisions for time keeping at: http://hea-www.harvard.edu/ECT/Daymarks/ called *Telling Time without a Clock: Scandinavian Daymarks.* The methods described in it are no doubt the same as used by the ancient Anglo-Saxons

Ritual Times

The earliest calendars of most ancient societies seem to have been established to keep track of religious observances. Agriculture, the other great preoccupation of ancient peoples had no real need for a calendar as the time to plant or reap was fairly obvious by observing the weather. Bede mentions several potential Anglo-Saxon holytides but did not unfortunately elaborate on them. Snorri does say if the Old Norse in the *Heimskringla* that:

þâ skyldi blôta î môti vetri til ârs, enn at miðjum vetri blôta til grôðrar, it þriðja at sumri, þat var sigrblôt

"On winter day there should be blood-sacrifice for a good year, and in the middle of winter for a good crop; and the third sacrifice should be on summer day, for victory in battle." (Ynglinga Saga Chapter 8)

The ancient Anglo-Saxon Heathens seem to have paralleled these three great holy tides of the Norse. Libermann in *The National Assembly in the Anglo-Saxon Period* notes that the Anglo-Saxon *witanagemót* met most often on St. Martin's Day (November 10th), Christmas, and Easter or Whitsunday. These dates correspond to when Anglo-Saxon kings are reported to have worn their crowns (Chaney, *Cult of Anglo-Saxon Kingship, p. 65*). If we accept Bede's description of the Anglo-Saxon pagan calendar in *De Temporum Ratione* there may have been more Anglo-Saxon pagan holy tides. Bede as stated above started the Heathen year with *Modranect*, the "Mothers Night." It fell between *Ærra Geola*, our December and *Æfterra Geola*, or January, and is the period today we know as Yule (which is now no more than a synonym for Christmas for most people). Of *Solmonað*, roughly our February, Bede says the Anglo-Saxons offered cakes to their Gods, and thus it was named the month of cakes; he also mentions *Hreðmonað*, roughly our March as when the Goddess *Hreðe* was worshipped, followed by *Eastremonað* when the Goddess *Eostre* was worshipped. He does not name *Liða* as a sacred month, however, that Midsummer falls within it, there may have been a holy day corresponding to Mid-Winter or Yule. This is pretty much confirmed by Midsummer celebrations that survived into modern times in England, not to mention much folklore surrounding St. John's Day which falls near the summer solstice. Bede then mentions *Haligmonað*, roughly our September, which was called "holy" as in Bede's words "because our ancestors, when they were heathen, paid their devil tribute in that month." The next potential holy tide mentioned by Bede is *Blótmonað*, roughly our November. The name its self means "sacrifice month" and was the time when animals were slaughtered for the coming winter. It follows *Winterfylleð* which corresponds to the Norse Winter Nights or Winter's Day, the time the ancients reckoned winter to have started. That All Hallows, St. Mar-

145

tin's Day, and Guy Fawkes Day, all important English holidays fall in this period would seem to indicate the actual holy tide took place near or at the junction of the two months. One of the problems in reconstructing the Anglo-Saxon Heathen calendar is that we do not know the criteria for dating a holy tide year to year with the exception of *Modranect* (and of course if we accept a similar holy tide on Midsummer). Heathen Easter for example may have been dated by the Spring equinox, the same way the Christian Easter is by the first Full Moon after the spring equinox, or by the first New Moon of Spring.

A Reconstruction of the Heathen Anglo-Saxon Calendar

A reliable reconstruction of the Heathen Anglo-Saxon calendar is possible (though whether it comes close to how the ancient one was truly reckoned is another matter). First we must make some assumptions based on Bede as we have few facts on how the calendar operated. These assumptions are: a. the month began on the First Crescent of the New Moon; b. the month was a synodic month; c. leap months were periodically used to pull the lunar calendar back in line with the solar year; d. the months of *Liþa* and *Giuli* are double months (that is they are roughly 57 days long). The first two assumptions are based on comparisons with other cultures that use a lunar or solar lunar calendar, the last two based on the statements by Bede on the month of *Þriliða* and the names of the months. In addition we a clue provided by Bede as to how the calendar should operate. *Modranect* is a set solar event that will not change year from year and therefore the calendar must accommodate it in some way. In order to make a solar lunar calendar work, we must first make up for the difference between the lunar and solar years. A lunar year using synodic months is 354 days long while a solar year is about 365. Using straight lunar months with no leap days, weeks, or months would result in the calendar being off by over an entire month in under four years. The Muslim calendar does this, allowing its months and holy tides to float around the year. However, as indicated by Bede (as well as the month names) this does not seem to be the case for the Anglo-Saxons. Therefore one needs to use leap months to keep the two calendars (solar and lunar in line). One method that works for this is to use the Metonic Cycle. The Metonic cycle was discovered by Meton of Athens (about. 440 BCE) who noticed that 235 lunar months made up almost exactly 19 solar years. Thus phases of the Moon fall on exactly the same solar dates every 19 years. By adding *Þrilíða* in the 3rd, 6th, 8th, 11th, 14th, and 19th years of this cycle one can keep the lunar months roughly in line with the solar calendar. Another method developed by Professor Kenneth Harrison involved using the the *octaëteris* or *ogdoas.* The *octaëteris* or *ogdoas* is a span of eight years of 99 lunar months at the start of the Metonic cycle following the pattern of OOEOOEOE where O is an ordinary year and E is a leap year. This method follows roughly the same pattern as the one above only over a shorter period. John Robert Stone based on Harrison's model created several rules that perhaps are more practical. These are (quoted exactly): 1. The next month is intercalary if the first crescent of the after *Líða* is observed on or before July 4, the eleventh evening after Midsummer Eve (June

23). 2. The next month is intercalary if the first crescent of the after *Liða* is observed before Midsummer. 3. The next summer will contain a third *Liða* if the first crescent of the after *Geola* is observed within the eves of Christmastide (December 24 to January 4). Stone's method does work but it also has problems. The first is he is working on the idea of an *Ærra Géola* and *Æftera Géola* as well as *Ærra Liða* and *Æftera Liða.* Bede does not mention these month names, and while the names for *Géola* are paralleled in the Gothic month names of *Fruma Jiuleis* and *Aftuma Jiulea,* there is little else to suggest these were separate months and not double months. The primary problem with using *Ærra Géola*, *Æftera Géola* and *Ærra Liða*, *Æftera Liða* is it is near impossible to construct a calendar that will sandwich the solar dates of Yule and Midsummer between their respective months. This is perhaps only possible if one uses double months for *Líþa* and *Giuli.* The Norse once used a calendar of only six 59 day months (or double months) which indicates the idea was not alien to Germanic peoples. If one makes *Líþa* and *Giuli* double months, one can then ensure that Yule and Midsummer always fall within their respective months regardless of which set of rules one uses. The next problem is reconciling the start of the year with the beginning of the months. Bede clearly states that the year began on *Módraniht* and gives a date of December 25th, the old winter solstice date under the Julian calendar. It is not truly possible for the first month of the year to begin on this date every year as the First Crescent of the New Moon will not fall on December 25th each and every year. Indeed, the majority of the time the First Crescent will not fall on December 25th. We

148

must assume then that perhaps Bede was mistaken, and that *Módraniht* merely fell near the start of the new month (perhaps within 12 days of it). It is also possible that the Anglo-Saxon new year was actually in the Fall, and that it began with *Winterfylleþ.* The Norse started their year at this time and referred to it as *Veturnætur* or "Winter Nights." In closing one can create a reconstruction by considering the following:

1) *Líþa* and *Giuli* are considered double months.

2) *Módraniht* fell within 12 nights of the First Crescent of the New Moon.

3) Intercalatory months were added in the 3rd, 6th, 8th, 11th, 14th, and 19th years of the Metonic Cycle.

Bibliography

Baity E.C. *Archaeoastronomy and Ethnoastronomy so far // Current Anthropology. 1973, 14. p.389-449.*

Harrison, Kenneth, *The Framework of Anglo-Saxon History to A.D. 900* Cambridge: Cambridge University Press 1976

Hastrup, Kirsten, *Culture and History in Medieval Iceland.* Oxford: Claredon Press 1985

Hutton, Ronald *The Pagan Religions of the Ancient British Isles; Their Nature and Legacy*

Nilsson, Martin P. *Primitive time-reckoning*, Lund: C. W. K. Gleerup, 1920

Straižys, Vytautas and Klimka, Libertas (12, Vilnius 2600)   *Chapter 5. Natural rythms and calendar, COSMOLOGY OF THE ANCIENT BALTS* Retrieved 2 Sept., 2004 from http://www.lithuanian.net/mitai/cosmos/baltai5.htm

Stone, John Robert, *Observing Bede's Anglo-Saxon Calendar* Retrieved 2, Sept., 2004 from http://www.kami.demon.co.uk/gesithas/calendar/obs_bede.html

Theodish Websites

Axenthof Thiad
http://www.axenthof.org/

Miercinga Theod
http://www.ealdriht.org

New Anglia Theod
http://www.newangliatheod.org/

Sahsisk Thíod
http://www.sahsisk.org/

Made in the USA
Charleston, SC
10 May 2012